Huimin Jin
Active Audience

Cultural Studies | The series is edited by Rainer Winter | Volume 41

Huimin Jin (PhD) is 211 Chair Professor of Cultural Theory & Aesthetics at Shanghai International Studies University, Shanghai, and Professor of Literary Theory at the Chinese Academy of Social Sciences, Beijing, China. His publications, among others, include *Post-Confucian Turn* (2008), *Consequences of New Media: A Critical Theory Concerning the End of Literature* (2005), *Postmodernity and Dialectical Hermeneutics* (2002), *Beyond the Will: A Study of Arthur Schopenhauer's Philosophy and Aesthetics* (1999 & 2007), and *Anti-Metaphysics and Contemporary Aesthetics* (1997). He is Editor of the journal *Differences* (Kaifeng: Henan University Press, 2002).

HUIMIN JIN
Active Audience
A New Materialistic Interpretation of a Key Concept
of Cultural Studies

[transcript]

Bibliographic information published by the Deutsche Nationalbibliothek
The Deutsche Nationalbibliothek lists this publication in the Deutsche Nationalbibliografie; detailed bibliographic data are available in the internet at http://dnb.d-nb.de

© **2012 transcript Verlag, Bielefeld**

All rights reserved. No part of this book may be reprinted or reproduced or utilized in any form or by any electronic, mechanical, or other means, now known or hereafter invented, including photocopying and recording, or in any information storage or retrieval system, without permission in writing from the publisher.

Cover concept: Kordula Röckenhaus, Bielefeld
Cover illustration: »directionless« (stockwerk23 / photocase.com) (Detail)
Typeset by Alexander Masch, Justine Haida, Bielefeld
Printed by Majuskel Medienproduktion GmbH, Wetzlar
ISBN 978-3-8376-1896-9

Contents

Foreword | 7

Acknowledgements | 11

Preface | 13

Introduction | 23

Chapter One. The Audience as Discursive Subject | 29

Chapter Two. Struggling out of the Iron House of Discourse | 45

Chapter Three. Towards a New Materialistic Conception of Audiences | 79

Coda: Chinese Examples | 115

Appendix 1. Towards Global Dialogism
Transcending 'Cultural Imperialism' and Its Critics | 119
1. Globalization as a New Philosophy | 119
2. The 'Globality' Cultural Studies
   in the Era of Globalization | 123
3. The 'Postmodernity' Cultural Studies
   Doesn't Acknowledge 'Cultural Imperialism' | 125
4. Where There Is the 'Modernity' Cultural Studies,
   There Is 'Cultural Imperialism' | 133

Conclusion: Towards Global Dialogism | 139
Notes | 141
References | 142

Appendix 2. British Cultural Studies, Active Audiences and the Status of Cultural Theory
An Interview with Professor David Morley | 145
References | 171
Acknowledgements | 172

About the Author | 173

Index | 175

Foreword

Since the 1970s, cultural studies has played a leading role in establishing and generating critically and sociologically oriented media studies, in the context of which the works of David Morley feature prominently. Following Stuart Hall's conceptual and theoretical works, and closely combining analytical reflections with empirical research, Morley has laid a firm foundation for the sociology of reception. His works serve as a highly important referential point for qualitative-ethnographic investigations into the media world, and also for research into the dynamic relations between local contexts and global influences, or, for an understanding of the social changes conditioned by media or media technology. Morley is now read world-widely and discussed vigorously as well.

However, there have so far been little philosophical discussion of the significance and relevance of this form of media studies. It is regrettable that traditionally a philosophical study has largely been absent in the field of cultural studies. This may be ascribed to the fact that cultural studies sees its own methodological approach basically as a *bricolage*. The theoretical positions and methods at hand are adapted and synthesised in order to analyse actual social and cultural problems. The purpose of cultural studies is therefore not the development of a general theory of culture or society but the political intervention, underpinned by theories or empirical research, with the aim to gain greater degrees of democracy and social justice. This view of theory, both reflexive and practical, which clearly distinguishes cultural studies from other approaches, is based upon the pedagogic and socio-political considerations that are connected to the emergence and formation of cultural studies in the context of *New Left* in the 1950s. Nevertheless, the philosophical, sociological, and even aesthetical contextualisation, systematisation, and development of the ideas, connections and requisites of cultural studies are needed and will be very helpful, with which we could better learn from cultural studies and contribute to its development.

Considered in this context, the present book by the Chinese cultural theorist Huimin Jin is extremely valuable and deserves warm congratulations. Professor Jin is an outstanding expert in philosophical hermeneutics and reception theory. He is also one of the most important representatives of cultural studies in China. He has made many presentations in international conferences held in various countries, and published articles in the journal *Theory, Culture and Society* (London *et al.*: Sage Publications) for which he serves as an associate editor. He made various efforts, distinguished and detailed, to expose the latent philosophical problematic in David Morley's media studies via an exploration of its origins and principles. His profound knowledge, especially of German philosophy, and his special perspective developed from Confucius, have led to a reading of Morley's work which considers him as a classic whose ideas are not fully comprehended and applied.

More importantly, Professor Jin suggests a new materialistic conception of active audiences, with which he is trying to show that the experience, practice and *Eigensinn* (making their own sense) of audiences will not be properly understood if one limits himself to the discursive level only. We must investigate what the ground is for audiences, what hides from them, or more precisely, what resistance means to them. The models for and the interlocutors with Jin are Schopenhauer, Freud, Lacan and Heidegger who have foregrounded the bodily *Trieb* and pre-linguistic unconscious of the 'Being-in-the-World', the defining role of which is exhibited. The sociologist Morley did not debate on these authors intensively enough; he wrote little about them. Professor Jin ennobles his Morley, positioning him in a rank of those discursive ground-breakers who are still powerfully relevant today.

With an extraordinary hermeneutic sensibility Huimin Jin opens and discloses a new orientation or perspective. I hope his book of complex and thoughtful argumentation will interest readers. And it remains for us to hope that the philosophical dimensions of cultural studies will attract more attention in the future.

Rainer Winter
Klagenfurt at Wörthersee, July 2011

Acknowledgements

I am greatly honoured by Professor Dr. Rainer Winter who has included the present book into his prestigious series 'Cultural Studies' published with transcript over the years, and I am deeply grateful to him for his kind review of my manuscript and warmly encouraging comments on it.

The critiques from Professor Ryan Bishop of the University of Southampton, who helped me to draft a book proposal for the manuscript, Professor Mike Featherstone, who published the last chapter in his internationally respected journal *Theory, Culture & Society* (vol. 28), and Professor Shaobo Xie at the University of Calgary, Canada, who discussed with me the main argument of the manuscript, have contributed a great deal to 'Preface', parts of which can be read as a response to their inspiring interrogation and/or suggestion. I appreciate these critiques, though, which does not mean I agree to every point of them.

Professor Xiaoping Wang of Capital Normal University provided the translation draft of the main part of this book. The same case is with the chapter 'Towards Global Dialogism', a translation draft of which was made by Dr. Min Zhou of Shanghai International Studies University. Thanks for their work! However, they will bear no responsibility for any errors or inadequacies that remain in the book, since I reworked their translation drafts and added a certain number of new materials and thoughts to them. Professor Ellen Zhang of Hong Kong Baptist University reviewed the manuscript and gave her valuable advice, especially concerning its English style. This translation was supported by the Chinese Academy of Social Sciences (Beijing), my home institution, a home, which has maternally nourished me bodily, intellectually and spiritually since 1984.

I owe a great debt to Shanghai International Studies University with which I have been affiliated since 2009 as 211 Chair Professor, the post of which encourages me to publish more abroad in English as well as in German—that is exactly what I have been looking forward to for long. Thanks, therefore, to Professor Jianhua Yu, Professor Deming Cao and Professor Shuguang Zhang of the University who have offered me the opportunity of honour and delight, by which I could realise my *Wunsch*.

Last but not the least important, my thanks and appreciation should be voiced to Ms. Jennifer Niediek and Mr. Kai Reinhardt at transcript Verlag, both of whom have tried their every effort to make the manuscript into a better product for readers as well as for the author.

Dr. Haiyan Chen, my father, if he were still alive, would be very happy to see the book, in English, and of his son!

H. J.
Beijing, August 17, 2012

Preface

June 2006, when the authorities of the University of Birmingham removed, abruptly yet resolutely, 'cultural studies', which, as a discipline though trans-disciplinary, had existed since the foundation of the Centre for Contemporary Cultural Studies (CCCS) in 1964, from their list of departments, is not a summer as it was in the natural sequence of seasons, but a winter which felt chilly for scholars of cultural studies, especially for those alumni and alumnae who were practicing and developing the model/s of cultural studies created by the so-called Birmingham School. The removal is absolutely no mere action of 'restructuring' a department as the university declared, but signals a collapse of a 'sacred temple', a spiritual and emotional hometown, to which scholars of cultural studies, no matter where they lived, believed they were belonging. However, from my point of view, this event is not necessarily an obituary of cultural studies as read by many. Rather, it should be understood as *a better turn* for cultural studies, since the closedown of a 'centre' is itself an act of *decentering*, wherein lies an objective of cultural studies. As John Hartley remarked, cultural studies is 'a philosophy of plenty', a spirit of differences, and of being marginal, regional, and critical.[1] If Hartley is not wrong, then a death of a 'centre' as happened in Birmingham would be most welcome by such cultural studies. When cultural studies becomes ubiquitous with various projects of its own, is a 'center', which always functions as a commander, still possible and necessary?

---

1 | See John Hartley, *A Short History of Cultural Studies*, London: Sage, 2003, p. 10.

Indeed, cultural studies has already been transnationalised and unniversalised, with numerous departments or programs established, with a plenty of books and articles brought out, and with conferences held domestically or internationally one after another; and what is more important, perspectives or theories of cultural studies have been widely applied to the humanities and social sciences, and the 'cultural studies unconscious', coined after Fredric Jameson's term the 'political unconscious', is on the way, just like a propitious rain, as quoted from Du Fu, a poet sage in the Tang Dynasty, which, 'With the wind, slips secretly into the night, /Silent and soft, moistens the world.' A 'centre' fell down in Birmingham, but countless centres have stood up elsewhere, which look like, to use a traditional Chinese metaphor, 'bamboos after a spring rain', wildly growing with greater vitality. Cultural studies, as far as it is concerned as an intellectual space, is not closed; quite the opposite, it is now being opened up with infinite possibilities.

However, retrospection is needed for cultural studies before it goes any further, the necessity of which arises from the fact that for every step forward in the humanities, there must be three steps backwards first and that what is gained must be at the cost of something lost. This is a reflexive claim which defines the humanities. One may criticise it as nostalgia, but for the humanities, nostalgia is not just a look back but by which a look forward is made in a way. Cultural studies has achieved a great deal over the last decades and will, as it looks, achieve more in the future; however, it should not be ignored that cultural studies, as many other movements, are also full of bubbles and baubles, sound and fury, and opportunism and commercialism. In this context, if cultural studies would like to go further, even a bit, or negatively speaking, if it is not willing to die of, still in Du Fu's poetic words, 'The happy craziness with which to roughly pack up all the books of poetry'[2], it needs then a kind of reflection and contemplation.

---

2 | The significance of the 'books of poetry' in traditional Chinese context is much like what Matthew Arnold suggests by his saying 'the best that is

We would better halt for a while, looking over our shoulder or walking backwards a bit, to check if there is anything lost when we are moving straightforward. More concretely for the topic of this text, we would better make a retrospective reading of the past cultural studies. As a mater of fact, cultural studies has never ceased to make reflections upon itself, and has never forgotten to look backwards at the traces it left. Needless to mention in between what have been done, which are too many to be put into consideration, we only refer back to Raymond Williams' essay 'The Future of Cultural Studies' (1989)[3], and also forward to a most recent one, a namesake with Williams' but a book, *Die Zukunft der Cultural Studies*[4], edited by Rainer Winter, and to be printed in July 2011. How coincidental they are! Or, the truth may be that Winter has been inspired by Williams. But anyhow, both of them indicate a reflexive consciousness which has never gone with the development of cultural studies.

Viewed this way, my book will be also a retrospective endeavor, with an aim to critically look backwards at British cultural studies, its history and theoretical legacy.

Among their best books of this kind are Graeme Turner's *British Cultural Studies* (1st ed. in 1990, and 2nd ed. in 1996) and John Hartley's *A Short History of Cultural Studies* (2003). The former is trying to provide an overview of British cultural studies, and comments in depth on the central categories as well, while the latter, revealing a genealogy of British cultural studies though, is basically

---

thought and said'. Du Fu's verse is borrowed here to indicate a spectacle of cultural studies in which the elite culture, poetry in particular, is thrown away and scholars turn to crazily dive into the study of popular culture that features the *carnivalesque* with which Mikhail Bakhtin has described the medieval popular culture.

3 | Raymond Williams, 'The Future of Cultural Studies', in his *Politics of Modernism, Against the New Conformists*, London & New York: Verso, 2007 [1989], pp. 151-162.

4 | Rainer Winter (ed.), *Die Zukunft der Cultural Studies, Theorie, Kultur und Gesellschaft im 21. Jarhundert*, Bielefeld: transcript, 2011.

a guide to the field of cultural studies in general. Besides, historical accounts of British cultural studies are also found in introductory works to cultural studies like, to name just a few, Chris Barker's *Cultural Studies: Theory and Practice* (2000), Simon During's *Cultural Studies: A Critical Introduction* (2005), John Storey's *Cultural studies and the Study of Popular Culture* (1996), and Fred Inglis' *Cultural Studies* (1993).

Despite a large number of retrospective works on/of cultural studies, there has been up to now no such one in a book form as dedicating itself exclusively to the study of one specific theoretical issue of it in the English speaking world. My book hopefully will be a pioneer, since it for the first time investigates into a particular theory of British cultural studies, i.e., *active audience theory*.

British cultural studies has of course many theoretical achievements, among which, however, active audience theory should be a defining one, by which I do not mean to say that British cultural studies is defined as and *is* active audience theory. The notion of 'culture industry' of the Frankfurt School has *already* won a worldwide currency with the logo of Critical Theory *for many years*; the notion of 'active audiences' of the Birmingham School, though paralleled in theoretical importance with the notion of 'culture industry', has not received the recognition it deserves with the worldwide movement of Cultural Studies. Too many attentions have been paid to 'culture industry', and too many people, especially Marxist critics, have accepted the definition of mass culture as culture industry of capitalism; but the related issues at stake remain unexplored concerning how capitalist mass culture is modified and resisted, and how capitalist discourse and its hegemonic structure are deconstructed by audiences. This book deals with, clarifying and interrogating, these issues, and in so doing, it is intended to establish a monument for active audience theory. We do not have to cancel the notion of 'culture industry' by wholesale, but we will insist that without active audience theory, the 'cognitive mapping' (Fredric Jameson) of mass culture would be incomplete and insufficient. Both 'active audiences' and 'culture industry' are needed, and they will make '*supplément*' (Jacques Derrida) to, but not substitute, each other. Only by this way can a complete map of mass culture be expected.

One may grumble that active audience theory is nothing but an old tale in the 70-80s of last century. As for this kind of complaints, I would like to give a warning that nothing will be outdated in the humanities which feature reflexivity, especially in the field of philosophy: as Hegel has taught us, the owl of Minerva takes its flight only when the shades of night are gathering. The night for active audience theory is coming right now.

More importantly, this book is far beyond a 'cognitive mapping' of active audience theory as it was. It speaks its own theory, it is a creative interpretation of, and has taken a further step from, the latter. To judge whether a theory is outdated or not is to see if it is still addressing us. Active audience theory, at least for the moment, still has something to tell us, and still bears some relevance to us. Of course, after 30 years or so when the theory was produced, we now have to say for it, of it yet, and certainly, more than it, since it is 'classic', past yet last.

It should be acknowledged that active audience theory is an epoch-making contribution by the Birmingham School to television studies, and if, broadly speaking, i.e., from the viewpoint of the study of popular culture, it should be as well a significant break-through with the notion of 'culture industry' held by the Frankfurt School. Nowadays active audience theory is employed as one of the primary treasures of British cultural studies, and regarded as one of the fundamentals in contemporary communication studies. Be it as it may, a kernel question why audiences are active has not been given, in the last analysis, a philosophical answer either by Stuart Hall or David Morley as its principal advocates. To speak frankly therefore, active audience theory is only halfway yet to its completion. By critically reviewing Hall's model of encoding/decoding, and especially by a close reading of Morley's ethnographic studies of audiences and the theoretical elucidations accompanied with them, this book has excluded all the ways to find the active audience in the direction of discourse as suggested by Hall in particular, and Morley in one way or another, and turned to develop a socio-ontological concept of audiences. This concept assumes that it is just because of its socio-ontological existence that the audience could have the activeness that is rendered eminent by the *resistance*; or, with a ring of Marx and Freud, the *material existence* of audiences serves as the last word to its activeness and resistance. Perhaps the argument here will be questioned for radicalising and therefore running off the track of active audience theory, but as defended by Karl Marx, 'To be radical is to grasp the matter by the root'[5], and the root of the matter, as I understand it, is the life-existence of man.

This is the point where we differ from Morley: it is with 'everyday life' that Morley stops but we depart; we go further to strip away the costumes of discourse, ideology, 'way', 'routine', and 'everyday' from 'everyday life', leaving the barely material existence of everyday life, the life that has not been culturised, the life in itself, as the last line of defense.

But how can the 'material existence' resist actively? One may remind us of that the 'material' is not any far from 'the masses' of 'culture industry' though they are of course not synonymous. Answers to this will vary according to the way in which the term 'active' is defined. In this book, we talk about the notion of 'active' ontologically, tracing the active force of 'the masses' farthest back to their unchangeable 'material existence'. But if so, anaesthetisation and deception, say, of mass culture, would be then *naturally* impossible; and given this, why do intellectuals bother to worry at all? The fact is that the material does *voice* its resistance, murmuring, moaning, sobbing and howling, for example, although such voice has not crystallised itself into discourse or ideology. And to make its voice, the material may, in some cases, *appropriate* the existing discourse or ideology, which seems to many as if it had discourse or ideology. The voice of literature has been long misunderstood as an ideology, for

---

5 | Karl Marx, 'Towards a Critique of Hegel's *Philosophy of Right*: Introduction', in David McLellan (ed.), *Karl Marx: Selected Writings*, Oxford: Oxford University Press, 1977, p. 69.

instance, by Luis Althusser, Terry Eagleton, and most Chinese critics, who believe that literature is an aesthetic ideology. There is a long way for a voice to become a discourse, so intellectuals are needed, who have the duties to listen to various voices and transform them into discourses, since only when transformed into a discourse, can a voice be effective to realise itself.

That we insist upon the active resistance of 'the masses' as 'material existence' is connected with and strongly supported by a supposition that matter has/is energy, as physics holds. One may follow the Frankfurt School, viewing the 'audience' as 'the masses', but s/he can not necessarily go as even to assert that 'the masses' are passive. 'The masses' have/are energy, and they exist actively, of which theorists of the Frankfurt School have no idea, and although well informed with Marxism, they fail to apply Marxist materialism to their speculations on the audience. To conceptualise 'the masses' as being passive is a misrepresentation of 'the masses'. As Raymond Williams remarks, 'There are in fact no masses; there are only ways of seeing people as masses.'[6]

Sociology of the audience perhaps does not need a philosophical version of active audience theory which can not be applied directly to those ethnographic investigations it usually makes into social contexts in which television is watched. I will not complain that Morley, as basically a sociologist of media, has not fully developed this version, nor will I do to his rebuke of my work in which sociology gives way to biology that, he insists, does not make sense in audience studies[7]. Nevertheless, there are three points I have to briefly make in

---

6 | Raymond Williams, *Culture and Society, 1780-1950*, New York: Columbia University Press, 1983 [1958], p. 298.

7 | At 'The Symposium on Contemporary Active Audiences and Cultural Studies' held by the University of International Business and Trade on Nov. 8th, 2010, the author gave a speech on 'Modernity and Postmodernity of British Cultural Studies'. Morley cast his doubts on the author's philosophical approach to active audiences and believed that the author was replacing sociology with biology.

defence: first, far from leaving behind the discursive and sociological studies of audiences, a philosophical version of active audiences as I am trying to draft will bring forth and give prominence to a dynamic relationship between the *discourse* and the *material existence* of audiences in a given *society*; second, it will drive scholars of audience studies to pay more attention to how the material existence of audiences shapes the 'way' of their daily life and the way of their 'discourse'; and third, to mention once again, we talk about the resistance ontologically, and if a biological force is ontologically the final determinant, it will be no longer merely biological but philosophical *déjà*.

'Resistance', as a topic generated in social theory many years ago, should not be accused of obsolescence. Quite the contrary, it is a topic of ever-increasing urgency with the global asymmetry as debates on climate exchange show, and with economic and cultural imperialism arising from globalisation that still does not come to an end for the moment. In China, for instance, 'resistance' is a complicated paradox. On the one hand, China, which has been ideologically disadvantaged since the times of 1840 when the Opium Wars broke out, has to resist the Western ideology, a capitalist ideology, in order to protect and reinforce its indigenous ideology, Confucianism, for instance; on the other hand, China, which has been highly motivated to modernise itself in order to catch up with the currents of the world, has to resist its traditional cultural forces, social values and norms in everyday life, in which context the Western discourses such as 'sciences' and 'democracy', which were called respectively 'Mr. Saï' and 'Mr. De' in the era of the May Fourth Movement (1919), and the trinity of 'Liberty, Equality, and Fraternity', are employed by the intellectual elites. More recent examples, among others, are the big split of New Left and New Right in China since the 1990s, and the half embrace and half skepticism with which Chinese official media meet 'universal values'.

In contrast to the domestic relevance of active audience theory when it was forged in its beginning years, the chapter 'Towards a Global Dialogism' as an appendix to this book is intended to transfer the discussion of 'resistance' into a global context in which the debate on 'cultural imperialism' was motivated in the 1960's and has been kept in the agenda of cultural politics till now. This transference does not originate with the author; Hall and Morley have initiated it much earlier, as this chapter shows. In his recent speech in Beijing, Morley once again emphasised the relevance of active audience theory to a global context.[8] Not devoted exclusively to the topic of resistance which, though, underpins it, what this chapter is trying to do chiefly is to divide, according to the arguments about 'cultural imperialism', cultural studies into two models, the modern and the post-modern; and with a hope to transcend the dichotomy, it then advocates a third one: global cultural studies. The spirit of this model is 'global dialogism', which holds simultaneously the singularity of interlocutors which can not be thoroughly penetrated and the transcendence of it only with which can a dialogue really happen. Obviously, this 'transcendence' is required essentially by dialogism; and if so, the word 'global' will be then just an intensifying description of that 'dialogism'. Besides these academic pursuits in this chapter, I also suggest a philosophical solution to the conflicts among civilisations in the contemporary world.

My interview with Morley, which is also included as an appendix, makes more visible and vivid my dialogue with Morley which has been already undertaken in the previous part of the book. However, this is not to say that Morley gives in the interview a clearer and friendlier restatement of his work, or even an authoritative endorsement, as one may expect, to my study of his work. I take Morley's response to my questions as, in a poststructuralist sense, a *text*, the inclusion of which will shed another light on my arguments and certainly leave them more or less in an insecure situation, but the same will happen with Morley's text. This is what 'intertextuality' suggests to us: in the context of 'intertextuality' there is no authoritative meaning that has been often misunderstood as the author's intention which, however, will be open to ever renewed interpretations by other texts.

---

8 | David Morley, 'Media Theory, Cultural Consumption, and the Changes of Technology', delivered in 'The 2010 BLCU Forum', Nov. 7th, 2010, Beijing.

A book will never be complete in a sense that it is unable to include everything relevant into its body. This book is no exception. It, for instance, leaves substantially untouched a pre-history of active audience theory, say, the works of Richard Hoggart and Raymond Williams (It is just in a note where this prehistory is mentioned), and neither has it brought into focus the contemporary contributions from other scholars like Ien Ang and John Fiske, to name the most prominent. We regret this. It is the fate of a book, which is always yet to be finished. But, *being yet to be finished* suggests, on the other hand, more meanings that are to be produced by others in the future. As its topic is on the active audience, this book should leave more blanks, even though we do not know yet the blanks it has left will be productive or not. This is not the author's saying but the readers'. Therefore, I'd better stop here for readers to step.

Introduction

With cultural studies spreading across the world, 'British cultural studies', or more accurately, the so-called Birmingham School, is increasingly received as one of the best traditions of that kind. However, it is still no easier matter to define 'British Cultural studies', even for such an expert as Professor John Storey, for instance, who is well-known for his good knowledge of how British cultural studies has come to be what it is today. Storey understood only too well that 'Cultural studies is not a monolithic body of theories and methods'[1], just as Stuart Hall pointed out, 'Cultural studies has multiple discourses; it has a number of different histories. It has a whole set of formations; it has its own different conjunctures and moments in the past. It included many different kinds of work. [...] It had many trajectories.' And in this sense, had he not maltreated himself, Hall even claimed that 'the theoretical work of the Center for Contemporary Cultural Studies' (CCCS) of Birmingham, led by him, was not a chorus of the octave harmonious melody, but, should be 'more appropriately called theoretical noise'.[2]

Kind of timid and doubtful as Storey was when he associated British Cultural Studies with the works of Richard Hoggart, Raymond Williams, E. P. Thompson, Hall, and so on, he was actually

---

1 | John Storey, *Cultural Studies and the Study of Popular Culture*, 2nd edition, Edinburgh: Edinburgh University Press, 2003, p. 1.

2 | Stuart Hall, 'Cultural Studies and Its Theoretical Legacies', in David Morley and Kuan-Hsing Chen (eds.), *Stuart Hall: Critical Dialogues in Cultural Studies*, London & New York: Routledge, 2005 [1996], p. 263.

quite assured and had given a clear-cut answer to such an undecided question—if seriously considered—as 'What is British cultural studies'. We could savor this between his lines in the passage that follows, and we would perceive that and we must say of many twists and exquisite parts, he had made careful and insightful observations:

If we are in search of a founding moment when cultural studies first emerges from left-Leavisism, 'pessimistic' versions of Marxism, American mass communication models, culturalism and structuralism, the publication of Stuart Hall's 'Encoding and Decoding in the Television Discourse' (Hall 1980; first published in 1973) is perhaps it.[3]

If we could not argue that Storey here had taken Hall's drafting of decoding and encoding paradigm as the *début* of British cultural studies, which seems not matching the widely recognised accounts of that history as we know it[4], then on the second thought, there is no

---

3 | John Storey, *Cultural Studies and the Study of Popular Culture*, p. 9. Stuart Hall's article 'Encoding and Decoding in the Television Discourse' (1973) that the quotation refers to was revised and retitled as 'Encoding/Decoding' (1980). This book uses the revised edition, and when the old version is used, the original title will be accordingly referred to.

4 | The books such as *The Uses of Literacy* (Richard Hoggart, 1957), *Culture and Society* (Raymond Williams, 1958), *The Long Revolution* (Raymond Williams, 1961), and *The Making of the English Working Class* (E. P. Thompson, 1963) are recognised by Stuart Hall as 'founding' and 'originating' texts of British cultural studies (See Stuart Hall, 'Cultural Studies and the Centre: Some Problematics and Problems', in S. Hall, D. Hobson, A. Lowe and P. Willis [eds], *Culture, Media, Language*, London: Hutchinson, 1981 [1980], p.16 and p. 278). However, this should not mean that they are the headwaters of cultural studies in any sense. As reminded by Raymond Williams, courses of cultural studies were conducted as early as in the late 1940's in army education or even in the 1930's in adult education. The only problem Williams felt sad with was that those people who were active in that field at that time did not

doubt, at least, that he had marked Hall's work as a new start-point of British cultural studies: This is the beginning of Hall's times of British cultural studies. If we can switch our perspective, for instance, picking out the most representative one from the beat spectrum in the field of British cultural studies and we find this has to be Stuart Hall actually, then we can certainly claim further that it was Hall who inaugurated the long lasting influential British cultural studies with his programmatic research on television discourse. No exaggeration to speak, Hall is British cultural studies! Before Hall, it was just a prehistory of British cultural studies. In other words, British cultural studies began with Hall.

David Morley (1945-), born with the times, luckily caught up with this great turning point of history. As a student of Hall, he was assigned to do cultural studies of television. In 1974, he wrote a course paper, but a seminal work as proved later on, titled 'reconceptualising the Media Audience: Towards an Ethnography of Audiences'. And since then, he has been running on this road of audience studies without stop and has published one after another the works such as *The 'Nationwide' Audience* (1980), *Family Television* (1986), and *Television, Audiences and Cultural Studies* (1992), etc., all of which are now read as classical in the field of television studies, and with which he is regarded as a major representative of the 'Active Audience Theory'. Even in a broader sense, i.e., in the field of communication and media studies, he could have no sense of shame to stand among the handful of the masters.

Hall's status as the chief designer of British cultural studies should not be called into question at any moment, but if not succeeded by Morley's continuous, lasting, deepening and systematic intensification and extension, Hall's idea about encoding and decoding, for instance, would remain nothing but a blueprint, notwithstanding its undeniable merit. Morley accepted Hall, but perhaps what is more important, he realised Hall's model. Hall's

---

publish (see Raymond Williams, *Politics of Modernism, Against the New Conformists*, London & New York: Verso, 2007 [1989], pp. 154-155).

significance as a text was revealed, expanded and rendered in this process of realisation, with which then consummated as a magnificent master piece. To us, however, the most appealing was not Morley's realisation of Hall's idea, but some new theoretical themes derived from this realising process, no matter they were discovered, stressed, or neglected, or even decidedly rejected, abandoned by Morley. The text cannot be monopolised by its author; this was recognised both by Hall and Morley. Now it was just that this commonplace proposition, mostly associated with German reception-aesthetics, has been used on them—to read them mainly in a *negotiated* or even *oppositional* position, though the *dominant-hegemonic* will not be discarded totally, the result of which, as I wish heartedly, will not surprise or embarrass them. The textual meaning is always growing if not so wildly as unexpected.

It is intended in this book to expose and develop the theoretical dimensions of Morley's television audience studies. That may run counter to the principle of cultural studies which features not to produce theories but to borrow the existing theories as in the case of Hall, who once compared himself to a magpie, collecting materials anywhere but to build its own nest. What concerns cultural studies or Hall most is the specific use of theories. As a follower of Hall, Morley also held an attitude of 'pragmatism' if this term does not imply anything Philistine, who said: 'If a theory is useful, then it must be able to be put into use.' According to him, whether a theory is good or not is decided by how well it has been used; theories that cannot be used are certainly useless, ineffective, and unnecessary and should be abandoned.[5] In his agenda-setting 'Introduction' to

---

5 | See Huimin Jin, 'A Talk about British Cultural Studies: Listing to Stuart Hall', in *The Academic Journal of the Capital Normal University*, 2006, no. 5. David Morley almost repeated what Hall said about theories when I met him in his Goldsmith office on 13th December, 2005. Before meeting Morely, I had made an interview with Hall in the lounge of Hotel Russell, London, on 25th November, 2005. Both meetings were appointed by the British Academy.

Television, Audiences and Cultural Studies, Morley even mocked the cross-boundary travel of theory in the form of cartoon: 'higher levels of abstraction ("theory") can be sold in a more extensive (and not naturally specific) market, and thus tend towards both higher levels of profitability for the publisher, and a wider reputation for the theorist. In short, "theory" travels best.'[6]

Now that Morley was so annoyed by theories and then so opposed to treating cultural studies 'simply as "theory"'[7], he would certainly not object Graeme Turner's account of the achievement of *The 'Nationwide' Audience* in his *British Cultural Studies: An Introduction* which was placed as 'the first and remains the best of its kind'[8]; or, at least, Morley wouldn't have any objections to Turner who identified the empirical characteristics of Morley's research on television audiences:

> The 'Nationwide' Audience is an important book because it provides us with empirical evidence that the polysemy of the television text is not just a theoretical abstraction, but an active, verifiable and determinate characteristic. Morley's continuing body of work has greatly advanced our understanding of the social dimension of television discourses [...][9]

At a visible level, this is quite a faithful description of Morley's work which seemed to place 'empirical' evidence over 'theoretical' deduction in value. *The 'Nationwide' Audience* was no more than a field report of the audience's response to the evening journal program 'Nationwide'. Although concluded with the conceptualisation of the audience, it was just the checking and verifying of his tutor's encoding and decoding formula, almost without any new sense theoretically. If

---

6 | David Morley, *Television, Audiences and Cultural Studies*, London & New York: Routledge, 1992, p. 4.
7 | Ibid., p. 3.
8 | John Hartley's blurb for Graeme Turner, *British cultural studies*, 3rd edition, London: Routledge, 2003.
9 | Graeme Turner, *British cultural studies*, p. 113.

such is the case, to launch a research project on Morley's 'theory' would be just like climbing the tree to catch the fish, the method being entirely wrong. However, if we are not satisfied with the Morley at the visible level, but take the visibility as the starting point and move a few steps further, or use the visibility as the material, we will discover what can be hardly perceived, and create Morley's image as a theorist or even a philosopher. We don't want to stick a theory upon Morley, but hope to knit out a theory of Morley. It comes from Morley and still belongs to Morley. In this case, if we retrospect Turner's conclusive remark on Morley's work, we will cry foul for Morley for it limits Morley's achievement only in the scope of empirical research, and fails to make out the theoretical implications at the deeper level. Our research will show that Morley's theoretical significance just lies in his act of opposing 'theories', and his intentional avoiding and rejecting theories. He did have a theory, but which was a non-theory.

Turner underestimated or even denied Morley's theoretical achievement, but he had provided us with the clues to seek Morley's theoretical significance. The clues are 'television discourses' and their 'social dimension' as lying silently in the passage quoted above. Between these two key terms, but not in either of them independently, hide all the theoretical mysteries and the generating points of the active audience.

Now let's start with 'television discourses'!

Chapter One.
The Audience as Discursive Subject

The so-called 'television discourses', or in a slightly different form, *televisual discourse*, illustrated by Hall in his paper 'Encoding/Decoding', is basically meant treating television not as 'technology' but as 'ideology', not as 'medium' but as 'the message carried by the medium'. The nature of the message is 'discourse'. Put more clearly, in the vocabulary of Hall, though the term 'television discourses' has morphologically two parts: 'television' and 'discourses', which are separate but make up one unit—the discourses of television, it can be read, syntactically, as a thesis: Television is discourse, or in a condensed form, television as discourse. The code either encoded or decoded belongs to the same televisual discourse in the different stages of transmission. Apparently, Hall seemed very concerned about the loss and the gain of the televisual discourse in the process of communication. He proposed three decoding positions or methods frequently quoted in the history of cultural studies: *dominant-hegemonic, negotiated,* and *oppositional*. This perhaps marked the beginning of a new period in British cultural studies, just as Storey claimed, but no matter his basically abandoned *dominant* decoding or his highly proposed *negotiated* and *oppositional* ones, each of them is nothing but a *method* of treating a code or discourse, and the central issue could only be the code or discourse. Through the analysis and display of the three modes, Hall's intention apparently lies in the examining of discourse changes in the process of television transmission. To Hall, discourse is politics, is ideology and discourse transmission is thus filled with struggles for power. At the end of his paper, Hall finally pointed out the political nature of decoding:

One of the most significant political moments (they also coincide with crisis points within the broadcasting organisations themselves, for obvious reasons) is the point when events which are normally signified and decoded in a negotiated way begin to be given an oppositional reading. Here the 'politics of signification'—the struggle in discourse—is joined.[1]

In fact, Hall did not give any prominence to the 'politics of signification' *in the dominant decoding* but in which there also exists a political dynamics or tension, with no difference from that in the negotiated and oppositional ones. Though what Hall brought to the highest level is the oppositional reading, and then to a less high level the negotiated one, they just demonstrate the ever existing politics in a protruding way. The political nature of decoding has never changed; what has been changed is just its appearance to us.

From Hall's point of view, television as discourse has thus become the battle field of discourses inevitably; it is inherently determined by the linguistics the televisual broadcasting has to use. Hall pointed out: 'Reality exists outside language, but it is constantly mediated by and through language: And what we can know and say has to be produced in and through discourse. [...] Thus there is no intelligible discourse without the operation of a code.'[2] If following the teaching of Laozi, the father of Daoism, that 'No name, the beginning of Heaven and Earth; but name, the mother of ten thousands things', then we can even conclude: it was language that created the world, it was language that created humanity, and it was language that presented the world to us human beings. Gadamer found: 'In Greek the expression for word, *Onoma*, simultaneously means 'name', and especially proper name,

---

1 | S. Hall, 'Encoding/decoding', in S. Hall, D. Hobson, A. Lowe and P. Willis (eds.), *Culture, Media, Language*, London: Hutchinson, 1981 [1980], p. 138.
2 | Ibid., p. 131.

i.e., called name (Rufname).'³ Although the *name* is not equal to the *word* and the word is neither equal to the *language*, the name was perhaps the earliest generated word or language. It was the name as *Ruf*name that had magically called out the chaos, the unknown world, called it in front of the people of *Logos*. People then owned a named world, but at the same time lost the world in itself. Gadamer attempted to treat language as ontological Being like the world in itself, but this world forever accompanied and bound by language will not be the world in itself. As a world of language, it belongs to human beings. So his saying goes: 'The Being, which can be understood, is language.' (*Sein, das verstanden werden kann, ist Sprache.*)⁴ Instead of regarding this as his endeavour to make language ontological, we'd rather read it as the failure of this endeavour. To further elaborate, it can be read as the abortion of his grand project of philosophical hermeneutics in which there was his wild ambition as well timid prudence with which to arrange his points. Gadamer was certainly very reluctant, but had to go back to the dualism that he had strongly rejected, returning to the borderline between language and world, thus being able to find the interaction and unity of language and world at the joints of this dualism. The unity of language and world hypothesised by linguistic ontology as Gadamer promoted does not suggest that language is the Being *in itself*, but '*The Being, which can be understood*', i.e., the Being *in language*, beyond which, however, there is also the incomprehensible Being, a world that cannot be reached by language. To say it conversely, if the Being is understandable, then it must exist in the language or through the language, and in this sense, understanding is just language; there is no understanding without language. Coming to the television broadcasting specifically, this broadcasting is a form of understanding or language. Hall reminded us that we must pay

---

3 | Hans-Georg Gadamer, *Hermeneutik I, Wahrheit und Methode, Grundzüge einer philosophischen Hermeneutik*, Tübingen: J. C. B. Mohr (Paul, Siebeck, 1986), S. 409. The English translation mine.
4 | Ebd., S. 478. The English translation mine.

attention to 'the discursive form of the message' and its priority in broadcasting:

> A 'raw' historical event cannot, *in that form*, be transmitted by, say, a television newscast. Events can only be signified within the aural-visual forms of televisual discourse. In the moment when a historical event passes under the sign of discourse, it is subject to all the complex formal 'rules' by which language signifies. To put it paradoxically, the event must become a 'story' before it can become a *communicative event*. [...] The 'message form' is the necessary 'form of appearance' of the event in its passage from source to receiver.[5]

The 'event' occurred in reality must be narrated, encoded and represented, which means first becoming 'message form', becoming 'televisual discourse'; and then it can be transmitted, understood, and received. Television broadcasting abides by linguistic rules.

Hall made no distinction between language itself and the use of language, a *signi*fying practice. Language as a collective cultural source is different from the lively use of this source. But Hall is not to blame for this. We may simply make language a tool for communication beyond class and ideology as Stalin argued, or decide that the linguistic signs are simply the arbitrary combinations of the signifier and the signified as Saussure showed. At any time and under any circumstance, however, so long as we hand the language over to a specific group of people, or hand it over to the user, or take language as the product of people, then the language must be intentional and expressional. At the time when class struggles happen, when class gets thematised, and in the place where there are class distinctions, language also bears class character. The instrumental nature of language perhaps only belongs to its whole humanity; with its once lively-past having been filtered, it becomes the public heritage. But, language cannot live without its users. To Hall, perhaps it is fundamentally wrong

---

5 | S. Hall, 'Encoding/decoding', in S. Hall, D. Hobson, A. Lowe and P. Willis (eds.), *Culture, Media, Language*, p. 129.

to hypothesise a language itself which is not in a social act and not put into any other use. In fact, Hall was not concerned about the linguistic issue of language; his interest was in the political implication of language, and in the politics of representation. And if language can be considered as a kind of 'representation', Hall was then able to demonstrate freely to us the language as narration, as discourse, as ideology, and in short, the politics of linguistic meaning. This is because the 'representation' has presupposed the binary schema of the language and the world, based on which, questions like how and whether language can represent the world, and like whether the 'representation' is truthful and legitimate, have also been presupposed. 'Discursive "knowledge" is the product not of the transparent representation of the "real" in language but of the articulation of language on real relations and conditions.'[6] Hall contrasted 'transparent representation' and 'articulation' as oppositions and then brought us, in a roundabout way, into the endless saying of the real relations which are unsayable on the other hand. There is no 'transparent representation' of the world at all, and the signifier can never reach any specific object but another signifier, the so-called 'signified'. As a signifying practice, 'articulation' is an effort to approach, to grasp, and to identify with, the specific object. To the practitioner, this effort is to be rewarding; otherwise, the effort should not be made, yet at the same time, the effort is always supplemented, negotiated, and resisted by the 'articulation' from other sides; thus, although the so called 'articulation' or 'hegemony' is said to be the reconciliation and peaceful co-existence of various elements and their contradictions, it may actually be called 'persistence' of those elements to its highest degree, not relaxed for a moment. Signs or the 'representation' through signs has determined that the expressional 'articulation' or the articulating expression is all but endless 're-articulation' or 're-expression'. 'Discourse' itself implies the struggle of the discourse, the struggle for the truthfulness and legitimacy of its 'representation'. Similarly, 'televisual discourse' is also meant the struggle of the televisual discourse.

---

6 | Ibid., p. 131.

'Televisual discourse' is certainly different from 'literary discourse' which is made of linguistic signs. As Hall noted, 'televisual discourse' is the 'visual sign': 'this type of sign is less arbitrary than a linguistic sign: the linguistic sign, 'cow' possesses none of the properties of the thing represented, whereas the visual sign appears to possess some of those properties.'[7] Now that serving as the sign, it will certainly abide by the rules of the sign—representation. Hall pointed out: 'Since the visual discourse translates a three-dimensional world into two-dimensional planes, it cannot, of course, *be* the referent or concept it signifies. The dog in the film can bark but it cannot bite!'[8] Here implies that the 'visual sign' remains the sign, as clarified by him a bit later in the same text: 'Iconic signs are therefore *coded* signs too—even if the codes here work differently from those of other signs.'[9] Any sign can be 'encoded' and thematised. Hall held: 'There is no degree zero in language'[10] where all signs, linguistic or visual, are hot or cool, or in whatever temperature, but never without temperature. Icons, in as much as signs, are not dumb; they speak as well—thus happens the iconoclasm, for example.

By claiming the television is the discourse, Hall remained in the domain of the Frankfurt School's 'culture industry' or Baudrillard's 'simulacrum', no matter how laboriously he had stressed the openness and polysemy of the televisual discourse. The reason lies in that they were all sealed up within the media texts, though Hall was alert about the cracks in the text, while the Frankfurt School or Baudrillard just turned a blind eye. Therefore, the 'culture industry' of the 'televisual discourse' and 'simulacrum' hypothesized the absolute control of the text in the whole process of televising. For Adorno and Horkheimer, the capitalist 'mass culture' is essentially the 'culture industry'; it is not 'a culture that arises spontaneously from the masses themselves', neither a 'contemporary form of popular art', but a product 'manu-

---

7 | Ibid., p. 132.
8 | Ibid., p. 131.
9 | Ibid., pp. 131-132. Emphasis added.
10 | Ibid., p. 132.

factured more or less according to plan'. 'The culture industry intentionally integrates its consumers from above.' And thus there is no place for the audience in the course of production and consumption by the theoretical imagination of the 'culture industry': 'the masses are not primary, but secondary, they are an object of calculation; an appendage of the machinery. The consumer is not a king, as the 'culture industry' would have us believe, not its subject but its object.'[11] Also from the perspective of the priority of the text, Baudrillard even abandoned the concept of the masses. If the audience is usually defined as the receivers of messages, but the 'simulacrum' had already imploded the border between texts and their significations, and all texts are not referring anything but themselves, then the audience, whose role is basically as receivers, would accordingly disappear.[12] Baudrillard imagined a strange category of 'the masses' or 'the audience' that was not within the broadcasting process of media, characterized with 'silence' or 'disappearance'; were this the case, how can such masses, not entering media 'phenomenon' and 'experience', but just staying with itself, start a kind of challenge, resistance and subversion to the media simulacra?

Obviously, the theory of the simulacrum cannot answer this question, as it is too postmodern. And the Frankfurt School can neither suppose any form of the autonomy and critical spirit of the masses, as it is too modern. About the sociological implications of 'modernity' and post-modernity', Douglas Kellner told us: 'Baudrillard interprets modernity as a process of explosion of commodification, mechanization, technology and market relations, in contrast to postmodern society, which is the site of an *implosion* of all boundaries, regions and distinctions between high and low culture, appearance and

---

11 | Theodor W. Adorno, 'Culture Industry Reconsidered', in Adorno, *The Culture Industry, Selected Essays on Mass Culture*, ed. & with an introduction by J. M. Bernstein, London & New York: Routledge, 2001, pp. 98-99.
12 | See Jean Baudrillard, 'The Masses: The Implosion of the Social in the Media', in Mark Poster (ed.), *Jean Baudrillard, Selected Writings*, Stanford: Stanford University Press, 1996 [1988], pp. 207-219.

reality, and just about every other binary opposition maintained by traditional philosophy and social theory.'[13] The *explosion* suppresses the other under the tyranny of the subject, or integrates it into the totality of the subject, while the *implosion* simply dismisses the binary of the subject and the object/other, thus the removal of the other. No matter the 'explosion' or the 'implosion' is to the media texts, the consequence will be the same: the extinction of the audience. The Frankfurt School and Baudrillard have actually not conducted any significant research on the audience, and the same case is the American model of mass communication research and all the other linear theories of communication and media. For all of them, the audience is not worthy of a look; the message, or the content, or the text, is everything. What the text is, what the audience may be; the role of the audience in the broadcasting process can be neglected.

Hall does not deny the overall dominance of the 'encoding' in the process of televisual transmission, and the 'encoding' is discursive, ideological, and of political pragmatics. This is the case with Marxist critical theories of media. Hall is a 'guaranteed' Marxist in this respect, but what is not 'guaranteed' is that he is 'a populist' as well, assuming that the mass/audience has their own discourse for decoding. 'Televisual discourse' is not the patent of the encoders. Hall also gives the discursive ability and rights to the audience. The audience being involved in the broadcasting process is not the *tabula rasa*. He or she has been pre-constructed by the discourse and brings the discourse into his or her act of receiving. For his assumption that decoding is a link of independence at a certain degree, Hall has to presuppose a discursive subject of decoding that corresponds to the discursive subject of encoding. Otherwise, how can he or she negotiate with and resist against the encoder. Even in the dominant and linear communication as believed by other models, the audience is still supposed to have the ability to receive—this ability is trained and formed by the discourse—though in this case the encoder and the

---

13 | Douglas Kellner, *Jean Baudrillard: From Marxism to Postmodernism and Beyond*, Cambridge: Polity, 1989, p. 68.

decoder share the discourses. However, to be precise, they share the same discourse from the different positions or contexts. Sharing the same is always temporary.

Let's illustrate the Hall of this line with recourse to the accounts of 'enlightenment' by Kant and Zhu Xi, a Confucian philosopher in the Song Dynasty of China, which is a bit away but still kind of pertinent.

The 'enlightenment' is often taken as 'knowledge-giving'; that 'knowledge' is 'light' seems to make sense—but this is only the 'enlightenment' in its primary sense; speaking more deeply, the knowledge used to 'enlighten' can only be 'instrumental', and is just a path toward the real knowledge. The enlightenment thinker Kant held that man has the faculty of a priori knowledge. The 'enlightenment' is not to instill to man the knowledge or ability to know from outside, but to wake up that knowledge or ability that has been covered by something. In his article 'An Answer to the Question: What is Enlightenment?' Kant defined 'enlightenment' as the *'emergence from self-incurred immaturity'* or from 'the inability to use one's own understanding without the guidance of another'.[14]

The Confucian classic *University* (*Daxue*, which can be literally translated as 'Grand Learning') is straight to the point when it describes the nature of 'university', and this 'university' is just the 'enlightenment' in the Kantian sense. It alleges: 'The principle of the university is to enlighten the light virtue.' Zhu Xi had a note to this:

The 'university' is the learning of great man. The 'enlighten' is to give light to. The 'light virtue' means that man was born with the light virtue and therefore his mind is not dark and stuffy but just contains thousand reasons that can understand everything. When confined within his temper and lust, man becomes blind. However, the original light of man has never

---

14 | Immanuel Kant, *An Answer to the Question: What is Enlightenment?*, trans. H. B. Nisbet, London: Penguin Books, p. 1.

ceased. So learners should enlighten man according to what he sends forth, and restore his original state.[15]

According to Zhu Xi's interpretation, the so called 'university' is just to learn to be a 'great man' with an ideal Confucian personality. And the so called 'great man' is characterised with the pure, bright and brilliant virtue; the methodology of the 'university' is not to inject the virtue into the heart of man, but to draw away the thick clouds of temper and lust and make the virtuous sunlight shine brightly forever. The virtuous light is always there, and it is 'the original light', neither increasing nor decreasing, but always the same. For this reason, 'enlightenment' doesn't mean plus or minus something to the mind of a man, but to 'restore his original state', or, to 'restore his beginning nature'[16]. By the way, Kant's 'enlightenment' was to restore man's 'reason' while Zhu Xi's was to wake up man's 'virtue', the difference of which derives from the Oriental and Western cultures. Here we will not discuss the matter. What we want to say is: somewhat related to Hall, the interpretations of 'enlightenment' by Kant and Zhu Xi revealed to us that the receiver of discourse must also be essentially a discourse agent, no matter his discourse is the same as or different from the discourse of encoders. Otherwise, discourse communication would be impossible. 'Playing the *qin* [a traditional Chinese musical instrument] to the cow', as a Chinese saying suggests, means the failure of the communication for both sides—the player and the listener—since they don't share musically, and in our case, discursively.

Hall was conscious of this logic of communication that requires not only an encoding 'discursive subject' but also a decoding 'discursive subject'. He did not see the dominant encoding as propaganda and implantation, but adopted Gramsci's concept 'hegemony' and

---

15 | Zhu Xi, 'Daxue Zhangju' ('The Exegesis to *University*'), in his *Sishu Zhangju Jizhu (Collected Exegeses to the Four Books)*, Beijing: Chinese Books Press, 2006, p. 3.
16 | Ibid., p. 1.

took it as the sharing of some meanings and discourses. This means that the encoders and decoders have the same knowledge and values—as the term 'common sense' suggests—however, which are also immanent in them all. In the case of the 'negotiated' decoding, the discursive subject begins to present its specialties:

Decoding within the *negotiated version* contains a mixture of adaptive and oppositional elements: it acknowledges the legitimacy of the hegemonic definitions to make the grand significations (abstract), while, at a more restricted, situational (situated) level, it makes its own ground rules—it operates with exceptions to the rule. It accords the privileged position to the dominant definitions of events while reserving the right to make a more negotiated application to 'local conditions', to its own more *corporate* positions.[17]

Although abiding by the rules, the 'negotiated' decoding tends to adjust and revise the rules according to its specific and exceptional circumstances. And further, in the case of the 'oppositional codes', the discursive subject is not just special, but even reaches a degree as 'opposition' in which the discursive subject, after its periods of the 'dominant' and the 'negotiated', is finally pushed into an extremely protruding position: it protrudes itself extremely, and in the extreme it protrudes itself.

It was due to the hypothesis of the audience as the discursive subject, but not due to the discovery of the polysemy of television, that Hall could possibly expect the advent of 'a new and exciting phase in so-called audience research'[18]. Unfortunately, many are not clear about this point. Simon During, for instance, described the reason why the audience was thematised in the field of cultural studies in his *Cultural Studies: A Critical Introduction*:

The emphasis on the polysemy of television and the variety of modes and moods in which it was viewed led cultural studies in the late seventies to

---

17 | S. Hall, 'Encoding/decoding', in S. Hall, D. Hobson, A. Lowe and P. Willis (eds.), *Culture, Media, Language*, p. 137.
18 | Ibid., p. 131.

pay increasing attention to television viewers not as members of a massified audience but as (socio-culturally formed) individuals, not as 'cultural dupes' with limited powers to accept or reject television's meanings but as people living more or less attentively around the television set.[19]

The *Turn to the Audience* that occurred in television studies or broadly, media studies, in the late 1970's, for During, was inaugurated theoretically with the emphasis on how television is watched actually. Doubtlessly, this is an insightful view, and we will follow up on the issue later, but if we parallel the actual television-watching with the polysemy of television discourses or even prioritize the latter in consideration, we may fall into plausible reasoning. There are quite a few causes to televisional polysemy. Analysed briefly, there are two: one is the problem with expression; the other is that with audiences. Like one's shadow that always follows him or her, the television expressions are always accompanied by the non-expressions. What we said will never be exactly what we meant to say. On the other hand, if audiences are not the audiences that have been '*mass*ified' but independent individuals, then 'decoding' will not always obey 'encoding'. 'Decoders' and 'encoders' are not one and the same but substantially two even in the framework of 'hegemony' where their individualities may shrink but remain alive in some other forms. 'Decoders' and 'encoders' are not symmetric! Thus, in terms of the relationship between the polysemy of texts and the activities of reception, it is the reception that is relatively independent from the text, it is the particular position of reception, and it is the subjectivity of reception discourse that has made the text polysemic. It can be argued that it is the audience that produces the textual polysemy that is an effect of the audience. But it cannot be said reversely that the existence of the audience is entrusted by the polysemy of the text. Even if there is such a case that a text only has one single meaning, it may still generate multiple meanings to the audience. The audience is never as innocent as

---

19 | Simon During, *Cultural Studies: A Critical Introduction*, London & New York: Routledge, 2005, p. 116.

what the text hopes; it exists before and outside the text, and brings the 'pre-existence' and 'outside existence' into its interaction with the text. Perhaps what During meant is that the polysemy shown by the television message has lured scholars of cultural studies into thinking of the meaningful practice of independent and lively audiences. But from a logical point of view, the fact is that without the audience, there will be no televisual polysemy. Seeing the televisual polysemy and then investigating the role of the audience to it, the sequence of which looks natural but cannot alter the *logical* hypothesis: first, the audience, and then, the polysemy. Well, this point is so crucial to Hall that without the presupposition of the autonomy of the audience's discourse, his favourite decoding positions—negotiated and oppositional—would not have been established.[20]

Although we cannot say Hall did not realise this at all, but what we can be fairly certain is that Hall did not pay enough attention to it, not to mention to emphasise it. In his article 'Encoding and Decoding', the discourse of the audience was not referred to even once. Hall's focus was on how the encoded 'codes' were both controlled and revised in the process of broadcasting. As for what has made such changes or according to what the decoders make these changes, he never went into details. It seemed that when he was about to write, the words escaped. Take the 'oppositional code' for example. When Hall pointed out that decoders 'detotalizes the message in the preferred code in order to retotalize the message within some alternative framework of reference'[21], he seemed to indicate to us an 'alternative framework of reference' different from the 'preferred code', which

---

20 | On the other hand, Hall made his effort to identify the polysemy with the text; and for him, a text is structured polysemic, as shown by Roman Ingarten in his book, among others, *The Literary Work of Art* (trans. George G. Grabowicz, Evanston, Illinois: Northwestern University Press, 1973). Dialectically, the polysemy comes from the text itself as well as the concretisation of it by the reader.

21 | S. Hall, 'Encoding/decoding', in S. Hall, D. Hobson, A. Lowe and P. Willis (eds.), *Culture, Media, Language*, p. 138.

means there is a code that belongs to audiences themselves. This code, he suggests, 'we must call *an oppositional code*'[22]. Here again he seemed to have confirmed a separated audience code because of its oppositional position. But immediately in the text that follows, the substitution of 'an oppositional reading' for '*an oppositional code*', which means an equation of them two, returns the '*oppositional code*' to encoders: 'an oppositional reading' is made *to* the code of encoders, the text of encoders, although it has maintained the code of the decoders themselves in order to keep their *op-position* for reading. But in effect, the decoders' code is obscured by the encoders' code. Even if Hall still intends to keep decoders' code, his intention will be also diluted by the introduction of encoders' code. In fact, Hall was not motivated to highlight the independence of the audience's discourse.

In his article 'The Structured Communication of Events', written in 1965, and largely revised in 1981—please notice that the time of writing this paper both precedes and comes after the article 'Encoding and Decoding in Televisual Discourses' (1973)—we finally found Hall's direct account of the audience discourse:

Audiences, like broadcasters, also stand in their own (very different) positions, relations, and situations, have their own (again, different) relationship to power, to information, to sources, and bring *their* own frameworks of interpretation to bear in order to get a meaning, or *decode* the message.[23]

In the restatement—that follows the above quotation immediately—of the three positions of decoding originally assumed in 'Encoding and Decoding in Televisual Discourses', it is seen that the audience code has become a basic awareness of Hall. Even if in describing the dominant decoding, he also used the phrase 'their [the audience's]

---

22 | Ibid.

23 | Stuart Hall, 'The Structured Communication of Events', in David Potter et al. (eds.), *Society and Social Sciences: An Introduction*, London & Henley: Routledge & Kegan Paul in association with the Open University Press, 1981, p. 280.

framework of interpretation': 'they [audiences] align *their frameworks of interpretation* with those of the communicators, and decode within the dominant, preferred or "hegemonic" definition of events.'[24] But in such a case, the audience's code for interpretation does not have any special features of its own; at most it is just the code they carry with them; or, they share the code with encoders. The difference of Gramsci's 'hegemony' from Marx's 'ruling ideas' lies in the fact that it tends to walk away from the perspective of class but acknowledges the existence of social 'consensus' or 'common sense'.

Perhaps one would ask: now that Hall was aware of the audience discourse and the audience discourse was so crucial to the opening of a new period of audience studies, why was Hall so careless about it and allowed it to appear or hide from time to time, flickering by itself? This can be referred to a paradoxical mission of the media group guided by Hall at that time. On the one hand, Hall wanted 'to replace these too-simple notions with a more active conception of the "audience"', i.e., to replace 'the passive and undifferentiated conceptions of the "audience"',[25] while on the other hand, he was trying to understand the complex relationship between media and ideology, or, the ideological function of media, with Gramsci's 'hegemony' and Althusser's 'articulation' that was then developed by Laclau and himself.[26] The former attempted to produce such audience discourse as: the more independent, the better, and the (most) oppositional, the best; but the latter did not want and allow this independence and opposition to end in a 'societal' split; rather, it held that contradictions should be coordinated, gaps should be filled and struggles should be compromised. The ideological function of media was to make conjunct the various contradictions, gaps and struggles persuasively and discursively. Hall pointed out: 'Considered "sociologically", the modern mass media

---

24 | Ibid. Emphasis added.
25 | Stuart Hall, 'Introduction to Media Studies at the Centre', in S. Hall, D. Hobson, A. Lowe and P. Willis (eds.), *Culture, Media, Language*, p. 118.
26 | See Stuart Hall, 'Introduction to Media Studies at the Centre', in S. Hall, D. Hobson, A. Lowe and P. Willis (eds.), *Culture, Media, Language*, p. 121.

help to integrate the different regions, classes and cultures of a complex society like Britain', and viewed in this way, 'The only comparable institution in earlier times would have been the church'.[27]

Similar to the church, the function of media is to integrate, but to integrate simultaneously means difference, contrast, and antagonism. Because of this, Hall defined the process of mass communication as 'a "complex structure in dominance"'[28] in the opening passage of *Encoding/Decoding*. This was a structure defined by negotiation, in which Hall could not boundlessly extend the audience's autonomy and could not acknowledge a code without any restriction. This also means not to acknowledge ontologically the existence of audiences as the incommensurable single individuals. Confined at the level of discourse or ideology, at the level of the subject being structured by discourse or ideology, and at the level of seeking 'consensus' or 'common sense', Hall could not take this into account.[29]

In spite of all these, Hall still drafted a new agenda for audience studies by giving 'televisual discourse' to the audience. Even if this audience is not limitlessly active, it is a *complex* structure at least, and it is with the *complexity* only that the total legitimacy of media audience research can be constructed. The complex of the audience, as we have been proving, derives from the proposition that the audience has its own discourse or its 'own frameworks of interpretation'. But this is far from enough.

---

27 | Stuart Hall, 'The Structured Communication of Events', in David Potter et al. (eds.), *Society and Social Sciences: An Introduction*, p. 269.

28 | S. Hall, 'Encoding/decoding', in S. Hall, D. Hobson, A. Lowe and P. Willis (eds.), *Culture, Media, Language*, p. 128.

29 | Even after reviewing Morley's *Family Television*, Hall was still not able to recognise the socio-ontological significance of Morley's audience studies in which the television-watching was placed into a domestic context. By contrast with Morley, Hall was trying harder but failed to escape the shadow of Althusser's ideology. (See Stuart Hall, 'Introduction', in David Morley, *Family Television: Cultural Power and Domestic Leisure*, London: Comedia, 1986, pp. 7-10)

Chapter Two.
Struggling out of the Iron House of Discourse

In his 'Encoding/Decoding', Hall acknowledged that his three positions of decoding were just hypothetical and 'These need to be empirically tested and refined'[1]. As Storey found, 'This *in part* is the project of David Morley's *The 'Nationwide' Audience* (1980)—to test Hall's model, to see how individual interpretations of televisual texts relate to "social position".'[2] Not simply saying 'This is', but prudently adding 'in part' to qualify the statement, this fully illustrates that at the time when Storey treated Morley's audience research as a test of Hall's decoding model, he was also aware that Morley had furthered and exceeded Hall's theory *in some other parts*, or at least that, Morley had not just repeated Hall's theory at an empirical level, and he still had his own agenda. Unfortunately, Storey was pretty vague about this critical point. He did not pinpoint clearly *in what parts* Morley was different from Hall. For this reason, in his narrative of British cultural studies, it seemed that Morley was just living under the shadow of Hall, only as his student or disciple, with no theoretically advancing and renewing of audience studies.

---

[1] | S. Hall, 'Encoding/decoding', in S. Hall, D. Hobson, A. Lowe and P. Willis (eds.), *Culture, Media, Language*, p. 136.
[2] | John Storey, *Cultural Studies and the Study of Popular Culture*, p. 14. Emphasis added.

Perhaps this wrong impression should not be imputed to a researcher as Storey; Morley himself was partly responsible. In terms of its purpose, Morley's project to conduct the 'Nationwide' Audience studies, at the level of his theoretical awareness, was just to prove the polysemy of televisual massages that Hall had already explained clearly—'Messages encoded one way can always be read in a different way.'[3] Looking at his research framework, we will find he was just following Hall's three decoding modes, having never tried to hypothesise other frameworks. This tells us that at the beginning of his audience studies, Morley did not foresee the theoretical consequence that his empirical studies might have, and he did not have this expectation; later he did not have any ambition for theory, either; on the contrary, he had a lot of hostility toward theory. However, the result was just the opposite of his intention: it will be proved that although Morley's empirical and sociological research on the television audience did have its own values and meanings if in view of his agenda, and he knew he had completed his prescribed plan; but in the sense of what he was not aware of, he actually accomplished himself as an audience theorist and more strictly, his image as a philosopher of ontology. This is rightly the case described by an old Chinese saying: 'Wishing to have the flower but no flower at last; not wishing to have the willow but willows line by line.' Wishing or not wishing, as a matter of *fact*, the result just appears of its own course. But only with an adequate exposure will the fact like Morley's be seen.

It can be said that Morley had walked on the road of ontological philosophy ever since the time when he began to do his project the *'Nationwide'* audience studies that aimed to empirically test Hall's encoding/decoding model. The primary cause to his making such advancement, perhaps we may argue, was the method that he had adopted in his audience studies. This was the method of 'ethnography'

---

3 | David Morley, *The 'Nationwide' Audience: Structure and Decoding*, London: British Film Institute, 1980, p. 10.

that had been traditionally used by British cultural studies[4]. Simply

---

4 | Morley did not refer to Richard Hoggart in his main works on the active audience, which seemed that there was no such person as Richard Hoggart in relation to him, but in fact it was Hoggart with his *The Uses of Literacy* (1957) who, certainly among others, had created a paradigm to apply 'ethnography' into the research on readers and audiences and formed an ethnographic paradigm in the history of British cultural studies; and further, it was with ethnography that British audience studies might find out the individuality of audiences from the *massifying* media. Sue Owen, a specialist of Hoggart, points out: 'This is a central theme in *The Uses of Literacy*: to know working-class readers is to understand that they are not as easily influenced as is assumed.' (Sue Owen, 'Introduction', in Sue Owen (ed.), *Richard Hoggart and Cultural Studies*, Basingstoke: Palgrave Macmillan, 2008, p. 2) And Stuart Hall has recently begun to realise that 'the implied argument in *The Uses of Literacy* runs, working-class audiences are not empty vessels on which the middle classes and the mass media can project, *tabula rasa*, whatever they want. They are not simply the products of "false consciousness" or "cultural dopes" (Hall, 1981). They have a "culture" of their own which, though it may lack the sophistication and authority afforded by the literary tradition and is certainly not unified, is in its own way just as dense, complex and richly articulated, morally, as that of the educated classes. It follows that the effects of cultural products cannot be "read off" or inferred directly from the contents of what is produced for them to consume because to have "social effects" of any depth they must enter into and be in active negotiation with an already fully elaborated social and cultural worlds. Reading, in this sense, is always a cultural practice.' (Stuart Hall, 'Richard Hoggart, *The Uses of Literacy* and the Cultural Turn', in Sue Owen [ed.], *Richard Hoggart and Cultural Studies*, p. 24) Apparently, Hall has spotted some traces of the active audience in Hoggart's *The Uses of Literacy*, which is implied as well in his own encoding/decoding model. And he has also seen the significance of the ethnographic methodology Hoggart employed to the conceptual formation of the active audience. He reads Hoggart's *The Uses of Literacy* as a founding text for cultural studies, rather than just thinking him to have merely set

speaking, the characteristic of this method is to practically and engagingly investigate the real living conditions of people, observing how they produce cultural meanings from their material life. Some scholars have particularly alerted: the ethnographic research 'starts not with a text or a theory (though it is certainly theoretically informed and alert) but a social group—bikers, schoolboys, housewives—and observes their use of commodities and messages to produce cultures, meanings and interpretations'[5]. From a perspective of philosophy,

---

up the Centre for such studies: 'It is widely recognized that without Richard Hoggart, there would have been no Centre for cultural studies. It is not always so widely acknowledged that without *The Uses of Literacy* there would have been no cultural studies.' (Ibid., p. 20) This is an *overview* assessment, however, from which we may infer *in section* that Hoggart's *The Uses of Literacy* should be a *rehearsal* if not an *inauguration* of the active audience that came as the 'encoding/decoding' model 16 years later. To this inference, Hall wouldn't object, nor would Morley who practised and advanced Hall's encoding/decoding model.

By rehabilitating Hoggart as a founding father of British active audience studies, we don't mean to criticise Morley for his ignorance of and indifference to Hoggart—as observed by Owen, Hoggart has been consigned to oblivion for a long time in the UK, but attracts increasing attentions in recent years, being re-read and revived. The international conference 'Richard Hoggart: Culture and Criticism' sponsored by the Leeds Metropolitan University (July 10-11th, 2009) was one of the signs for the new trend—but to reaffirm that British cultural studies does have a tradition of active reading or active audiences. Of course, besides Hoggart, many other figures contributed in their own ways to the formation of this tradition, for instance, Raymond Williams, whose redefinition of 'culture' as way of ordinary life may be a more direct, more apparent, and more *acknowledged* force to Hall and Morley (See Stuart Hall, 'Richard Hoggart, *The Uses of Literacy* and the Cultural Turn', in Sue Owen (ed.), *Richard Hoggart and Cultural Studies*, pp. 20-32).

5 | Janet Batsleer, Tony Davies, Rebecca O'Rourke & Chris Weedon, *Rewriting English: Cultural Politics of Gender and Class*, London & New York: Methuen, 1985, p. 146.

ethnography as a methodology is not interested in an epistemology of the binary opposition between consciousness and its objects, but tends to ontologise and existentialise this consciousness, i.e., to think of it as part of life or reality. In terms of ethnography, although 'culture' may retain its intellectual and spiritual dimensions, it should never be just limited to such abstract things; a key point is: 'culture' belongs to a way of life, if there's anything abstract in it, it must mix with life, must exist in life, and must appear as life. Here we need to proclaim immediately that ethnographic 'culture' is not the realization of a cultural concept in a top-down manner. It is first and foremost a practice of life, only from which can the 'sublimation' in a Freudian sense—which is the so-called 'culture'—be imagined. Morley claimed the goal of his audience research is to establish 'ethnography of reading'. Method may not be everything, but the 'ethnographic' method that Morley had chosen really painted his research with a background color, which is sociological, realistic, and individual. In proving the audiences' different readings of the same television text and in making 'social position' as the main cause to generating the polysemy of a text, he was able to capture how 'social position' is revised by 'special discourse position': 'It is always a question of how social position plus particular discourse positions produce specific readings'[6]. To be clearer, the question is not so much concerned with the 'social position' as a grand framework in which readings occur, as the social classes and their positions are distinct, but with the negotiation of the 'special discourse positions' with the 'social position', which generates different readings. The 'special discourse positions' are situational, subject to the time and place, to the audience's concrete emotion, idea, experience, etc., so they are always changeable and unstable and yet to be determined. For instance, I clearly know my feeling of reading a text previously, but I cannot predict how I will read it the next time, for each reading is another reading. Confucius knows this very well, so he teaches: 'By reviewing the old can one gain knowledge of the new.' Morley emphasised the uniqueness of

---

6 | David Morley, *Television, Audiences and Cultural Studies*, p. 118.

reading. In 'Afterword' of his *The 'Nationwide' Audience*, he appeared quite modest, but actually persisted in and argued for his own points or orientations of audience theory:

> I have been able to do no more than to indicate some of the ways in which social position and (sub)cultural frameworks may be related to individual readings. To claim more than that, on the basis of such a small sample, would be misleading. Similarly, I would claim only to have shown the viability of an approach which treats the audience as a set of cultural groupings rather than as a mass of individuals or as a set of rigid socio-demographic categories. Clearly, more work needs to be done on the relation between group and individual readings.[7]

Morley did have an intention to make his audience studies different from Hall's, but this intention as seen in *The 'Nationwide' Audience* was not well realised in every part of it, not consistent, not clear enough and strong enough; and what is worse, it is weakened or checked by *what contradicts it* from time to time. In *The 'Nationwide' Audience*, that which contradicts his intention is the 'discourse'.

Just as shown above, Hall noticed the existence of audience 'discourse' and for this reason, decoding is able to become the negotiation or opposition between the text and the audience. This even includes the dominant reading process. Morley succeeded Hall's tele-

---

7 | David Morley, *The 'Nationwide' Audience: Structure and Decoding*, p. 163. John Storey quoted this passage and remarked that Morley treats his work 'rather too modestly' (See John Storey, *Cultural Studies and the Study of Popular Culture*, p. 17), but this is, in my opinion, just a rhetorical trick called 'making a concession in order to move forward', because in the next research Morley undertook, the concept 'individual readings' was not abandoned but developed into the readings *in a context*, say, in a domestic context, which defines readings. Storey may know this story quite well, but for him a hard question will be that: if Morley's modesty betrays his lack of confidence in the 'individual readings', why could Morley have been carrying on with what he is not confident in?

vision discourse theory. He took the text as a kind of discourse and implanted it into the audiences' discourses, letting these different discourses to face, to negotiate with, to conflict or to dominate each other: 'although their [the audience discourses'] action is simply more visible when it is a negative and contradictory rather than a positive and reinforcing effect.'[8] The audience discourse is always there, sometimes hidden sometimes appearing, sometimes strong sometimes weak, but having never disappeared. To illustrate this, Morley borrowed a *discursive subject*, as I would term it, from Althusser:

> We need to construct a model in which the social subject is always seen as interpellated by a number of discourses, some of which are in parallel and reinforce each other, some of which are contradictory and block or inflect the successful interpellation of the subject by other discourses. Positively or negatively, other discourses are always involved in the relation of text and subject, although their action is simply more visible when it is a negative and contradictory rather than a positive and reinforcing effect.[9]

To be a social subject, the audience must be interpellated by the text's discourse; or, as a fulfilled social subject, it must have experienced the interrogation of discourses, either textual or social. Althusser indicated for Morley the discourses' ubiquity and their completeness and thoroughness with which to construct the subject. Hence, the message broadcaster as the apparatus of ideology/discourse aims, by its nature, to construct the audience into the subject of ideology/discourse, or, to re-construct the audience into the new subject of their own ideology/discourse. Hall then revealed the complicatedness of the process of construction or reconstruction, but was still prisoned within the framework of Althusser because Hall regarded the communication just as the encounter of multiple discourses and the competing field of discourses. But when adopting Althusser's theory

---

8 | David Morley, *The 'Nationwide' Audience: Structure and Decoding*, p. 162.
9 | Ibid.

of ideology, Morley did not notice that if regarding the audience only as the subject interrogated and them formed by discourses, or in other words, regarding the audience only as the effect of discourses, and as fundamentally having no its own existence, no inner life, then this will just block the way to the active audience Morley had in mind. In his *Family Television* published in 1986, Morley finally realised that what Althusser had done with subject was nothing but to

> reduce our shop steward [which is concrete subject, and certainly, individual] to the status of a mere personification of a given structure [the collection of individual in which there is no individual authentically], 'spoken' by the discourses which cross the space of his subjectivity. However, it is not simply Althusser who is at issue here; much of the psychoanalytic work on the theory of ideology generates an equally passive notion of subjectivity, in which the subject is precisely "spoken" by the discourses which constitute *that person*.[10]

Contrarily to this, Morley attempted to 'formulate a position from which we can see the person actively producing meanings from the restricted range of cultural resources which his or her structural position has allowed them access to.'[11] The Althusserian 'subject' has not disengaged itself totally from a specific person; no, it always appears as 'that person' or 'this person' as Morley saw it, but 'that person' has never been 'that person' and 'this person' has never been 'this person', *en personne*, because, according to Althusser, '*all ideology interpellates the concrete individuals [les individus concrets] into concrete subjects [sujets concrets]*'[12]; in other words, '*all ideology has the function (which defines it) of "constituting" concrete individuals [des individus*

---

10 | David Morley, *Family Television: Cultural Power and Domestic Leisure*, London: Comedia, 1986, p. 43. Emphasis added.
11 | Ibid.
12 | Louis Althusser, *Positions (1964-1975)*, Paris: Editions Socials, 1976, p. 113. My translation.

concrets] into subjects'¹³. This is just the basic function of ideology, because of which, the seemingly concrete individuals or subjects are nothing but the shadows of ideology. Morley's active audience needs individuality or concreteness, while Althusser's ideological apparatus happens to have destructed this individuality or concreteness and therefore the concept of an independent and autonomous 'subject' as modern Western philosophy supposed. Everything is ideology and everything is discourse. As constituted ideologically and discursively, Althusser's 'subject' is only passive and is not active at all. Althusser's version of ideological subject will not support Morley's active audience, and even worse, it is nothing but a French version of the Frankfurt School's 'cultural industry': the 'ideological apparatus' is the 'cultural industry,' and the 'subject' is the passive 'masses'. Such a theory of subject can only support the dominant decoding in Hall's model, but in this case, the so-called 'subject' is then just *subject to* the dominant *encoding*.

Just as the ideological subject, the discursive subject as constituted discursively will not be the subject in its full sense. Discourses are not able to construct the subject; rather, they can only construct a false subject, a simulated subject, a feeling of subject that feels real and natural. Therefore, what is crucial to Hall, and more to Morley, is not the question of whether the audience can be a discourse of *one side*, a discourse of *the other* relative to that of the encoder, and a *special* discourse, but whether the discourse of the audience can still retain its nature as being one side, the other and the special after it has been constructed by discourse.

Following Hall's pathway, Morley always regarded communication as the communication of discourses. Compared with Hall, he made a more assured and more *refined* step. He borrowed the concept of 'interdiscourse' of Michel Pêcheux, a follower of Althusser, and the interpretation of this concept by R. Woods *et al.* as well¹⁴,

---

13 | Ibid., p. 110. My translation.
14 | We noticed that Morley had never referred directly to the definition and interpretation of the 'interdiscourse' made by Pêcheux himself, so the

thus defining the discourse communication as the 'interdiscourse' communication, which contained three layers of meaning as below:

First, the discourse or the media text itself was already made of and interwoven with multiple discourses in its very beginning. Before Morley, or perhaps for Morley if you like, Hall had acknowledged 'Television discourse' as a complex of various discourses when he observed how codes are encoded and decoded from the perspective of 'ideology' and from the perspective of 'ideology' revised by Gramsci's 'hegemony' and Laclau's 'articulation'. In his 'Encoding/Decoding', Hall pointed out:

---

following now should be given against the original text: Pêcheux put forward his thesis first: *'Every discursive formation, by the transparency of the meaning constituted in it, conceals its dependence on the "complex whole in dominance" of the discursive formations, itself imbricated with the complex of ideological formations'*, and then he elaborated: 'Let's expand this: we propose to call this "complex whole in dominance" of discursive formations as "interdiscourse", with the qualification that it too is subject to the law of unevenness-contradiction-subornation which I have described as characterising the complex of ideological formations.' (Michel Pêcheux, *Language, Semantics and Ideology*, trans. Harbans Nagpal, London & Basingstoke: Macmillan, 1982, p. 113. The English translation has been changed a bit in order to be more faithful to the French edition: Michel Pêcheux, *Les vérités de la Palice, linquistique, sémantique, philosophie*, Paris: François Maspero, 1975, p. 146)

To be more specific, the concept 'interdiscourse' consists of two points: first, any *parole* or discourse is predetermined by an ideological 'complex', an *Autre* (Lacan), or, a *Subjet* (Althusser), which is called, if in the terminology of Pêcheux, *'préconstruit'*. Second, however, the construction of the subject is also the *'articulation'* among all kinds of discourses, which is filled with contestations, concessions, fissures and sutures, but not a total control without any space for interplay. (See Michel Pêcheux, *Language, Semantics and Ideology*, pp. 113-129)

though the production structures of television originate the television discourse, they do not constitute a closed system. They draw topics, treatments, agendas, events, personnel, images of the audience, 'definitions of situation' from other sources and other discursive formations within the wider socio-cultural and political structure of which they are a differentiated part.[15]

Hall linked the discourse's production with its reception, and the encoding with the decoding: 'they are differentiated moments within the totality formed by the social relations of the communicative process as a whole.'[16] The 'totality' Hall referred to is not the removal or resolution of all the oppositions, all the contradictions, and all the others harshly criticised by the postmodernists such as Foucault, Derrida, and Levinas. It is not the 'end of history' fantasised by Hegelians or the utopian 'Great Oneness' flaunted by the ancient Chinese. Rather, this totality is an unstable and temporary alliance of various oppositions, contradictions and incommensurable others. It is an endless process rather than an established fact, and it is an effort that never ceases but never succeeds in realising the 'totality'. As neither a Hegelian nor a postmodernist, Hall picked up the concept of 'totality' conveniently but with the aim to describe the function of media as 'ideology' in a complicated society to integrate the different interest groups and their beliefs, concepts and cultures. But it was clear to Hall that this integration is not beyond various social relations; on the contrary, it is regulated and limited by a 'determinate structure'[17]. Hall exposed: 'On the whole, the media are scrupulously fair, impartial and "balanced" within the terms of reference of the consensus, as we (and they) have defined it. Thus, they are not, on the whole, "partial" to Government or Opposition Party. But they are 'partial' to the

---

15 | S. Hall, 'Encoding/decoding', in S. Hall, D. Hobson, A. Lowe and P. Willis (eds.), *Culture, Media, Language*, p. 129.
16 | Ibid., p. 130.
17 | Stuart Hall, 'The Structured Communication of Events', in David Potter et al. (eds.), *Society and Social Sciences: An Introduction*, p. 286.

system, and to the "definitions of political reality" which the system defines.'[18] For example, he said, the 'consensus' for media may allow Labour and Conservative to argue about an economic policy on the television. No matter how divided they are in opinion, 'they both subscribe to the two-party system.'[19] The 'consensus' is a paradox, which means the '"Consensus" depends on structured disagreement—all those shared premises which enable "Tweedledum and Tweedledee to *agree* to have a quarrel"'[20]. To Hall, when the 'consensus', which seems to get beyond all differences, falls into a 'determined structure', the media text will not lose its complexity and polysemy (most of which are produced by the audience as indicated earlier), but becomes even more complex and more polysemic. This is because the media text as the carrier of 'ideology' or 'discourse' has moved into a deeper level of the 'cracks' and 'articulations' of the society from the level of the 'consensus', integration, and balance, which are intentional, fictional, transcendent, and shallow, and beneath which there are the heterogeneities that have been suppressed, excluded, and ignored. But in fact, none of the heterogeneities may be wiped out. They are just vaguely accessed to the 'consensus' from a place that is unconscious, marginal, and under-grounded. They are the potential forces to change the dominant 'consensus'. No discourse is sealed; all the discourses have cracks and only because of these cracks, can the world and its authenticity, variety and diversity be revealed to us. On the whole, it is the existence of the heterogeneities and cracks that makes the discourse have the endless implications, the articulating power beyond our imagination, and the identity of the art text with the world. In his lecture 'The Origin of the Work of Art'[21], Heidegger suggested that it is in the works of art in which there are lots of cracks

---

18 | Ibid., p. 284.
19 | Ibid.
20 | Ibid.
21 | See Martin Heidegger, 'Der Ursprung des Kunstwerkes (1935/36)', in: id., *Holzwege*, Frankfurt am Main: Vittorio Klostermann, 2003 [1950], S. 1-74.

that we may see an unveiled world. The 'totality' picked up by Hall is not the unveiled truth of Heidegger, but still contains a few hints of socio-ontology; if it is not the discourse itself, it is, at least, the condition for all discourses.

The integrity and multiplicity of the encoder's discourse are the same as those of the decoder's discourse. If considering that the encoder and the decoder dwell in the same society, in the 'totality' of this society, regardless this 'totality' is a discursive system or a condition for discourses, then the concept of 'interdiscourse' employed by Morley will have its second meaning—multiplicity and integration, This is to say that even before the audience encounters the encoder's 'interdiscourse', before entering the television text interwoven by discourses, they have been already interwoven and constructed by discourses. The audience needs to be constructed yet, but it is a construct already. Of such an audience, Morley has his description: 'the individual viewer does not come to the moment of viewing "cultural naked"—he comes to the text carrying already, and thinking within, his own set of cultural codes and frameworks—derived from his social and cultural situation and background.'[22] Here Morley obviously thought of the *Vorsicht* and its other names such as *Vorhabe, Vorbegriff, Vorstruktur,* and *Vorentwurf,* all of which are considered ontological by the Heidegger-Gadamerian hermeneutics. In a place where Morley explained Pêcheux's 'interdiscourse', the living, existing and concrete features of '*Vorsicht*' were vividly represented on paper: 'we, as people existing in a field of different discourses, different message systems, are situated between those different systems. We experience a multiplicity of discourse'[23]. The discourse as the '*Vorsicht*', or simply, the discourse, is our existence, our life and our concreteness and reality. But the discourse as the '*Vorsicht*' and thus as the ontology of the discourse will not necessarily incline to or support Morley's 'active audience' or the activeness of the audience. In the works of Heidegger and Gadamer, the ontology of the '*Vorsicht*' implies a kind

---

22 | David Morley, *Television, Audiences and Cultural Studies*, p. 92.
23 | Ibid., p. 77.

of fatalism in culture and tradition, and also the legitimisation of culture and tradition. We have to understand culture and tradition within the defined culture and tradition that cannot be dismantled at will, say, by the Enlightenment, as prejudice and irrationality. We may expose the *Vorsicht* further with Althusser's conceptualisation of the '*idéologie*', or, vice versa. According to Althusser, the *idéologie* is a '*contrainte*', a '*préassignation*',[24] or, a pre-constrained and pre-assigned structure, which is ready to exert its formative force on concrete individuals before their birth. In such a sense, the *idéologie* is a synonym of the *Vorsicht*, and Heidegger's *Vorstruktur* suffices as well to replace Althusser's *idéologie*. However, the *idéologie* does not have a sense of 'fundamental ontology' as the *Vorsicht* and *Vorstruktur* with Heidegger and Gadamer. What Althusser emphasised of the *idéologie* are its abstraction, exteriority, and imaginariness as opposite to the concretenesss of individuals Althusser had comparatively neglected. As far as its *ubiquity* is concerned, the *idéologie* cannot part with ontology as revealed in Heidegger's *Vorsicht* and *Vorstruktur*, which are also ubiquitous. But the big difference is that the '*Vorsicht*' is the ontology of the '*Vorsicht*' itself, and is the independent existence of the '*Vorsicht*' itself; while the *idéologie* as ontology is the ontology outside the concrete individuals. The former can be called an '*immanent* ontology', and the latter a '*transcendent* ontology'; the former does not acknowledge individuals, for individuals melt into the '*Vorsicht*' of ontology, while the latter regards ideology and individuals as two kinds of independent, if not separate, existence. But both the former and the latter are trying to connect the 'subject' or the 'individual' or the media 'audience' with the '*Vorsicht*' or the 'ideology' or the 'discourse', i.e., with the whole 'world'. In the conception of the 'interdiscourse', the 'audience' is determined by the 'world,' and represents the complexity and totality of the 'world'. To Althusser, this 'world' is structured by 'ideology'; to Derrida, it is the 'text'; and to Foucault, it is the 'discourse'; but, it is never the world in itself. So long as the audience belongs to this 'world', their discourse must have been

---

24 | Louis Althusser, *Positions (1964-1975)*, p. 116.

interwoven with other discourses many times; it is one discourse in the 'world' of discourses, not only related to other discourses, but also formed and transformed by other discourses. The discourse is always already inter-related. Perhaps poststructuralism is right when it argues: the discourse is never the discourse of a real thing, but the discourse of a discourse; the discourse does not have its externality; outside the discourse there The third meaning of the 'interdiscourse' is the 'discourse' dialogue between encoders and decoders. It goes without saying that the 'communication' itself is 'dialogue', seeking for dialogue and believing in dialogue, regardless of whatever kind it may be. In the explanation of Morley, the 'interdiscourse' is first of all a dialogue at the level of discourse. He found that Althusser's 'subject is a discursive category'[25], and Laclau, following Althusser, put 'interpellation' 'at the level of the discourse'[26], and 'at the level of the play in and struggle over discourse'[27]. He learned from MacIntyre that 'the limits of action are the limits of description'[28], and this is to say, he explained, 'thinking is the selection and manipulation of "available" symbolic material'[29]. Therefore, he suggested, 'Language must be conceived of as exercising a determining influence on the problems of individual thought and action'[30]. The limits of language are the limits of thinking and action, if man is defined as the *rational animal only*. This argument seems to have dominated Western philosophy for a long time. Hall's encoding/decoding model, as analysed above, also takes the communication as an exchange of codes and discourses. Everything occurs between discourses, or fundamentally speaking, *within* discourse. The event cannot get beyond discourses.

---

25 | David Morley, *Television, Audiences and Cultural Studies*, p. 62.
26 | Ibid.
27 | Ibid., p. 63.
28 | Quoted in David Morley, *Television, Audiences and Cultural Studies*, p. 94.
29 | David Morley, *Television, Audiences and Cultural Studies*, p. 95.
30 | Ibid., p. 94.

In the sense of Hall, in the sense of Althusser and Laclau, and in the sense of Heidegger and Gadamer, Pêcheux's 'interdiscourse' cannot substantively produce for Morley the audience's activeness. Perhaps Morley should not bother to adopt the concept of 'interdiscourse', but it was the only theoretical source at hand for him. Only running at the level of discourse, making discourse absolute or, ontological, may put Morley, who was pursuing the active audience, in dire straits. Hall assured us of the independence of the audience, but failed to explain from where this independence would arise, and if audience discourse belongs to a certain class, a certain ideology, then it will be passive first of all and second, it may be simply categorised. This is obviously not in accordance with the diversified activities in the actual decoding practice.

Hall did not realise this problem or perhaps he believed his three positions of decoding are theoretically sufficient for audience studies. He didn't need the liveliness and the divergent differences. In his 'Encoding/Decoding', he was influenced by Althusser so heavily that one may not risk saying that he was neither more nor less than an Althusserian there. For instance, to those who think of 'reading' not only as the capacity to identify and decode a certain number of signs, but also as the 'subjective capacity' to creatively rearrange these signs and their relation with other signs, he was extraordinarily sensitive, although such a point of view is not any absurd in an ordinary eye. He was worried that the concept of 'subjective capacity' might mislead to thinking that 'as if the referent of a televisional discourse were an objective fact but the interpretative level were an individualised and private matter'[31]. He reminded us that:

Quite the opposite seems to be the case. Televisual practice takes 'objective' (that is, systemic) responsibility precisely for the relations which disparate signs contract with one another in any discursive instance, and

---

31 | S. Hall, 'Encoding/decoding', in S. Hall, D. Hobson, A. Lowe and P. Willis (eds.), *Culture, Media, Language*, p. 135.

thus continually rearranges, delimits and prescribes into what 'awareness of one's total environment' these items are arranged.[32]

Hall was not so naïve as being blind to the individual and private elements in the real activities of decoding. When discussing the use of 'selective perception' to explain the inconsistency between encoding and decoding, he still acknowledged that 'there will always be private, individual, variant readings'[33]; however, he immediately pointed out:

But 'selective perception' is almost never as selective, random or privatized as the concept suggests. The patterns exhibit, across individual variants, significant clusterings. Any new approach to audience studies will therefore have to begin with a critique of 'selective perception' theory.[34]

Following Althusser, Hall obviously placed the dominant reading in the center of communication, while marginalising the individual and various readings. This is the inevitable upshot of taking communication as a linguistic event in which only codes or discourses are exchanged. So long as within the threshold of codes or discourses, communication will not fail in principle because codes or discourses mean language, rationality and their clarity and purity, while the individuality and sensitivity are vague, complicated, and resisting interpretation. In other words, so long as you enunciate a *word*, I will definitely decode it with *reason*; if the word is written down as a text, then it may be further rendered as Derrida's 'trace'. This 'trace' is also reason, so ancient texts such as the Chinese Oracle Inscriptions can still be deciphered with reason. There is only one reason in the world, by which men, though living in different times, can understand and be connected with each other. However, according to Gadamer, as mentioned in previous chapter, '*The Being, which can be understood, is language.*' This is to say, only at the level of language or discourse can

---

32 | Ibid.
33 | Ibid.
34 | Ibid.

men understand each other. But, the language or discourse has to be associated with the thing in one way or another and the thing is the kernel that cannot be penetrated by them. The individual and private readings belong to this opaque kernel. Thus, the communication is never transparent and guaranteed, but always filled with ambiguities and misreadings.

Morley did not see Hall's problem, but he, intentionally or not, captured Althusser's problem that was in fact the same with Hall's. He quoted a passage from Althusser's article 'Ideology and Ideological State Apparatus':

> It is clear that this ideological constraint and pre-appointment, and all the rituals of rearing and then education in the family, have some relationship with what Freud studied in the forms of the pre-genital and genital 'stages' of sexuality, [...] But let us leave this point, too, on one side.[35]

Here, what Althusser talked about is the absoluteness or thoroughness of ideological function to the construction of subject, which goes to such an extent that even an unborn baby is 'assigné à l'être [assigned to the being]'[36] and configured by the specific familial ideology[37]. It will receive Lacan's 'le Nom du Père' (the Name of Father), it will have an identity, and it will therefore become irreplaceable. As for these pre-appointments and pre-constraints, Althusser assumed that 'The baby is always-already a subject before his or her birth'[38]. This shows that Althusser had pushed the ideology's function of subject-construction to its upper limit: it seems not very hard for us to accept the argument that the individual is always-already a subject, as the individual is the individual in the society, internalising and embodying the social values and norms; but it would sound a bit far-fetched if

---

35 | Quoted in David Morley, *Television, Audiences and Cultural Studies*, p. 62. See Louis Althusser, *Positions (1964-1975)*, p. 116.
36 | Louis Althusser, *Positions (1964-1975)*, p. 116.
37 | See ibid.
38 | Ibid., p. 115-116. My translation.

we say that an unborn baby has entered a system of ideology and has become the subject of ideology. In fact, the formation of subject is a process of turning from a non-subject into a subject, in which the subject begins with its being a non-subject, if the process has a start. Were this wrong, may we shift to another perspective: the subject always needs a heterogeneous non-subject to survive, having both dimensions of being subject and non-subject. Althusser noticed the non-subject dimension of a subject or, the existence of the non-subject yet to be a subject, which is, in Freud's terminology, the 'pre-genital' and 'genital stages' of sexuality, or put more simply, the unconscious, undivided and without 'I', —Morley's quotation has eliminated the words that further explain the *pre-genital* and *genital stages* of 'sexuality': 'i.e. in the "grip" of what Freud has identified [repéré], by its effects, as being the unconscious.'[39] But this does not really matter, as speaking of sexuality is substantially of the *instinct* (*Trieb*)[40] and *unconscious* or the like. What really matters is that although these are the sources of ideological subjects, they are not the ideological subjects themselves. More strictly speaking, they, by nature, resist the ideology; and although they will be constructed as subjects by the ideology, they will never be fully the subjects as the ideology hopes. To use the metaphor of 'ice berg', the subjects, in as much as they are subjects, are just the smaller part of the 'ice berg' that emerges out of water, while the non-subjects are the larger part of it that sinks into water. Why is it only 'by its effects' that Freud can grasp 'the unconscious'? This is because the unconscious for its being not conscious has nothing to do with appearance, yet we can only predict its existence from the traces it leaves in the preconscious or consciousness. In Freud's theory, there are two worlds that are assumed: the conscious world and the unconscious world. The former is controlled and finally determined by the

---

39 | Ibid., p. 116. My translation.

40 | Freud's German word 'Trieb' was translated into English as 'instinct', but it seems that 'instinctual drive', or simply, 'drive', is more accepted now. However, considering that there is a meaning of 'drive' originally in the word 'instinct', I keep alive 'instinct' throughout the text.

latter. For Lacan, by whom Althusser was deeply influenced, there is, quite similar to Freud's case, the distinction between the *réel* and the *symbolique*. The latter intends to represent and integrate the *réel*, while the *réel* refuses to be included into the 'Symbolic Order'. However, the *symbolique* never parts with the *réel*, and the *réel* is always the object that the *symbolique* is trying to clearly say about and to fully represent but fails to do so as ever. To Freud, the unconscious is beyond the reach of consciousness; and to Lacan, the *réel* is beyond the reach of the *symbolique*. Then to Althusser, when he became aware of the unconscious and the *réel* and their refusal to and escape from consciousness and the *symbolique* in the utmost sense, he should have already acknowledged that although ideology may do everything, it is not able to do whatever it wants; in other words, 'do everything' just means 'do *to* everything'. Metaphorically, the unconscious is the astronomical black hole where ideology is deformed and defunct. Althusser would certainly evade the unconscious like this, and he had no reason to include it into his theory of ideology. In fact, what interested Althusser of Freud and Lacan was not so much the unconscious or the *réel* in itself, but the linguistic structuration, the symbolic representation, the societal and cultural aspects, of the unconscious or the *réel*. In an article on Freud and Lacan, Althusser argued that it is 'a new science', which is *'linguistics'*, or to be more exactly, it is the *structuralist* linguistics, that throws a light upon the psychoanalysis of the unconscious.[41] He paralleled Freud with Lacan in linguistics: 'Freud himself said that everything depended on language. Lacan makes this more precise: "the discourse of the unconscious is structured like a language."'[42] He eulogised it 'the most original aspect of Lacan's work, his discovery' that the transition from purely biological existence to human existence is achieved within 'the Law of Order', and re-named this law as 'the Law of Culture'; and he was quite delighted to see that in Lacan 'this Law of Order is confounded in its *formal* essence with *the order of lang-*

---

41 | Louis Althusser, 'Prefatory Note to "Freud and Lacan"', in Perry Anderson (ed.), *New Left Review*, no. 55, May-June 1969, p. 58.
42 | Ibid.

uage.'⁴³ Doubtlessly, if in Lacan's terminology, these could be called 'the Law of the Symbolic' or 'the Symbolic Order' as well. Compared with Freud, Lacan was, as said, different in many ways; but Althusser did not show much interest in this; he paid his attention mainly to their consensus and confirmation about the linguistic dimension of the unconscious. The reason is obvious: the linguistic dimension of the unconscious will open a gateway for Althusser to his conception of ideology. But Althusser's conception of ideology did not fall under psychoanalysis or the unconscious: if following Lacan closely, he should have taken the unconscious as a discourse of ideology, a discourse of *l'Autre* that is beyond subject; and if getting closer to Freud, he should have inscribed the ideological 'trauma' into the primordial 'instinct'. Although his 'ideology' exists and functions everywhere, it has not entered the world of the Freudian *unconscious*; and therefore, we should not imitate, for example, Fredric Jameson⁴⁴, to equate Althusser's ideology with Heidegger's 'Being-in-the-world' that is ontological. To Althusser, neither ideology nor the 'political' is the unconscious: the 'political unconscious', or, the 'cultural unconscious', both of which were developed by Jameson, among others, can only be Lacanian and Freudian. Differently, the Althusserian ideology is a concept of epistemology. It may be *apparatus*ised, *materialised*, and put into *practice*, but essentially it is a *'représentation'* of the 'real conditions of exis-

---

43 | Ibid., p. 59. Emphasis added.
44 | The Althusserian *idéologie* was confounded with Heideggerian *In-der-Welt-sein* (Being-in-the-world) by Frederic Jameson when he was trying to distinguish *ideology* from *science*: 'Althusser has discarded the traditional form of the opposition between science and ideology. Science and scientific revolutions and discoveries take place on the epistemological level [...] while ideology is a function of everyday life and the choices and paths of individual navigating it. [...] Ideology is thus, to use a Heideggerian expression, our Being-in-the-world.' (Frederic Jameson, 'Introduction', in Louis Althusser, *Lenin and Philosophy and Other Essays*, New York: Monthly Review Press, 2001, pp. xiii-xiv)

tence'[45], it is imaginary and conceptual, and it cannot live independently but has to be nourished by something else or elsewhere. Althusser's 'Ideology and Ideological State Apparatuses (Notes toward an Investigation)' was completed in April, 1969, and a year later, in April, 1970, an excursus to it was added, in which Althusser had a clarification of, which was by no means a revision to but an insistence upon, his recognition of the imaginary and conceptual feature of ideology: 'the ideologies are not "born" in the *AIE* but from the social classes gripped in the class struggle: from their conditions of existence, their practices, their experiences of the struggle, etc.'[46] Although the *AIE* (*les appareils idéologiques d'Etat*) may suggest that 'The ideology has a material existence' and 'always exists in an apparatus, and its practice or practices. This existence is material'[47], but this 'apparatus', this 'practice' or these 'practices', to be concise, materiality, are actually nothing but 'la *réalisation* d'une idéologie'[48]: in which the material is just the *reification* or *embodiment* of, and with nothing substantially new added to, the ideology. The 'material existence' of the *AIE* can never be equated with the practices and experiences of the social classes and their life and struggle; there are three layers among them: the social existence (1) produces its social ideology (2), according to Marxism, and apart from existing as a *conceptual* system, the social ideology also needs to take a *material* form (3), as showed in the *AIE*. For this reason, when Althusser talked about ideology and its apparatuses that construct subject, he had tacitly assumed 'la "détermination en dernière instance" par la base économique'[49]. The problem with Althusser is: his ideology is an epistemological concept, and his subject is an effect of discourse within the domain of this ideology; and feeling no contradiction with this, he simultaneously placed into the depth of his ideology, the Marxist *base*, the Freudian *unconscious*, the Lacanian *réel*

---

45 | Louis Althusser, *Positions (1964-1975)*, p. 101.
46 | Ibid., p. 125. My translation.
47 | Ibid., p. 105. My translation.
48 | Ibid. Emphasis added.
49 | Ibid., p. 75.

and the like; however, he did not make both sides responded and corresponded to each other, which, as a consequence, seemed as if it was the ideology alone that constructed the subject, and as if the ideology was not only the beginning but also the end; or, like the almighty God, it created the beginning and accomplished the end. Then the subject is just a synonym of ideology, and if we follow one of his propositions that *'the ideology does not have a history'*[50], then the subject does not have a history either. Like the ideology, the subject has been hollowed out all of its reality and becomes a floating signifier as assumed by poststructuralism. Although Althusser also said that *'all ideology interpellates concrete individuals into concrete subjects'*[51], in which there does exist something like *concrete*ness, yet the subject's *concreteness* is no more than a piece of clothes for the body of ideology. The *individuals*, as far as they are *toujours-déjà* subjects, are 'toujours "abstraits"'[52], as contended by Althusser. If it can be supposed on the other hand that individuals are concrete in the very beginning, this only means that it is since the very beginning that they have been serving as a container of ideology. Ideology never acknowledges concreteness, and neither individuals in their full sense. What ideology does to individuals is just hollowing out their concreteness, and then filling them up with abstractions, discourses, or rather, the ideology itself, which is to say, transforming individuals into subjects, and into puppets of ideology.

Up to now, we have discussed Morley's criticism of Althusser who viewed subjects as constructed by ideology so as to make the audiences hollow, puppet-like, controlled and then passive; and we have also pointed out that if just importing into audience studies Pêcheux's 'interdiscourse' and Laclau's 'play in and struggle over discourse', both of which feature articulation/disarticulation between discourses, there would be no way for Morley to reach the concept of the active audience. By all the above, what we have clarified and accentuated is: if taking the route of discourse only, as showed by

---

50 | Ibid., p. 99. My translation.
51 | Ibid., p. 113. My translation.
52 | Ibid., p. 115.

Hall, there will be no authentic 'decoding', no negotiated or oppositional 'decoding', except the dominant 'decoding' if it can still be called 'decoding'—or rather, it should be called the reproduction of the codes encoded rather than 'decoding'; and there will be no Morley's *active audience* either. But, as it is clearly seen, although Morley was aware of the problem with the discourse, he had never abandoned the methodology of discourse or ideological discourse, which is typical of the Birmingham media studies. Not betraying the tradition of British cultural studies, Morley's active audience theory still walked along the discourse route set by Althusser. Morley was not trying to change the route; but innovatively, he mapped the 'social existence' as another route, and made it parallel with the discourse route, thus producing a tension between them. It was not to simply dismiss 'discourse' or 'interdiscourse', but to sophisticatedly make the 'social existence' as a background and also a discourse element imbedded into a discourse communication, enabling the dumb 'social existence' to speak in the process of 'interdiscourse'. Therefore, different from Pêcheux, the 'interdiscourse' appropriated by Morley was no longer a dialogue that appears at the level of discourse only, but a dialogue that is deeply rooted in the soil of 'social existence', which may still take a discursive form though. Morley did not *overtly* criticise Hall's discourse-centrism, but Althusser's; however, if it can be said that Morley had not abandoned Hall's discourse-centrism, then he did not abandon Althusser's ideology either, in spite of the fact that he criticised Althusser directly. Just like treating Hall's discourse, he placed 'social existence' into the ideological interpellation to subjects, which means as well to place 'social existence' into the dynamics of 'interdiscourse' in the formation of subjects.

It will be extremely difficult to make Morley leave discourse but argue for the 'social existence' only. Just as illustrated above, he quoted the passage from Althusser who put aside the Freudian *unconscious*, but read it in an opposite way to what we did above: we hold that the Freudian *unconscious* and Lacanian structured *unconscious*, which can be rendered as, if in Marxist terminology, the *social existence*, or the *economic base*, or the *practice* of class struggle, but were neglected by Althusser, *as a Marxist* (!), are the final limits of the impact made by ideological discourses upon subjects, and the never dried-up sources of energy, fed by which the audience can launch the most powerful challenge and resistance to textual discourses or 'cultural industry'. But Morley did just oppositely. He felt it fortunate that Althusser only wrote superficially about the unconscious, and did not take it seriously. He regarded that both Althusser and those psychoanalysis-dominated theories, 'Screen theory', for instance, hold a view of determinism on the formation of subjects. It is truly the case, say, for Althusser, as we exposed it previously, who insisted that all individuals are always-already subjects: they are structured, and they are nothing less than the structure, and as the pre-determinant for subjects, the structure may be Freud's unconscious, or, Lacan's language (as the unconscious). For Althusser, it was indeed a long standing project to *deconstruct* the modern conception of the subject with structure, more precisely, with his *structured* ideological analysis, as disclosed in an essay drafted in January 1964 (corrected in February 1969), much earlier than he wrote his 'Ideology and Ideological State Apparatuses':

Since Copernicus, we have known that the earth is not the 'centre' of the universe. Since Marx, we have known that the human subject, the economic, political or philosophical ego is not the 'centre' of history—and even, in opposition to the Philosophers of the Enlightenment and to Hegel, that history has no 'centre' but possesses a structure which has no necessary 'centre' except in ideological misrecognition. In turn, Freud has discovered for us that the real subject, the individual in his unique essence, has not the form of an 'ego', centred on the 'ego', on 'consciousness' or on 'existence'—whether this is the existence of the for-itself, of the body-proper or of 'behaviour'—that the human subject is de-centred, constituted by a structure which has no centre either, except in the imaginary misrecognition of the 'ego', i.e., in the ideological formations in which it 'recognizes' itself.[53]

---

53 | Louis Althusser, 'Prefatory Note to "Freud and Lacan"', in Perry Anderson (ed.), *New Left Review*, no. 55, May-June 1969, pp. 64-65.

According to this narrative by Althusser, there was, in the history of Western thoughts, a long tradition of the subject-deconstruction, which should not be just associated with the French structuralism as we usually imagined it, but can be traced back to those figures who were as old as Copernicus, Marx, Freud, and to which Lacan will be no exception either if we may notice how Lacan was restated by Althusser in an earlier passage of this article, for instance: 'what Lacan calls the Symbolic Order, the order of objectifying language, which will finally allow him [the child] to say: I, you, he, she or it, and which will therefore allow the small child to situate itself as *a human child* in a world of adult thirds'[54]. Proud as he might be, Althusser implied that his ideological theory was certainly part of this 'Copernican Revolution' which characteristically transformed the modern subject that determines into the postmodern one that is determined, or in other words, which relegated the subject.

Morley did not like this post-modern determinism that had involved Althusser and psychoanalysis. But what delighted him was that he discovered, to take a metaphor, a crack in the seemingly airless and dark room of Althusser's ideological determinism. Although Morley could not re-sculpture the passive Althusser into an active Althusser with this crack, yet at least he saw thereby a dim light for the prisoned subjects to escape. This crack appeared in the place of 'interpellation': 'The term "interpellation" itself is an ambiguous one and has been subject to variable formations.'[55] On the one hand, Morley admitted, the 'interpellation' indicates that 'the subject is a discursive category'[56]; on the other hand, he captured Althusser's supplement that followed immediately: '*the category of the subject is only constitutive of all ideology in so far as ideology has the function (which defines it) of*

---

[54] | Ibid., p. 60. The quotation is slightly revised against Louis Althusser, *Positions [1964-1975]*, p. 25. The 'third' means 'Father', the presence of whom adds a third party to the child and its mother.
[55] | David Morley, *Television, Audiences and Cultural Studies*, p. 62.
[56] | Ibid.

"*constituting*" *concrete individuals as subjects.*'⁵⁷ The key words here are 'function' and 'concrete': the 'function' or 'interpellation' of ideology always points to 'concrete' individuals, situated in and therefore affected by a concrete context; or it may even be asserted, as Morley quoted from Althusser, that 'there is no ideology except for concrete subjects'⁵⁸. This is to say, there is no general and abstract ideology, but only the one that exercises its function *concretely*. And because of the *concrete*, ideology cannot fully realise, or, copy, itself onto the subject. From this concreteness, Morley saw a dynamic, fluid, and changeful ideological 'interpellation'. This suggests to Morley, not to us, that there is no need to abandon discourse or ideology, but so long as placing it into a concrete situation, he could transform Althusser's passive subject into the active audience.

As argued previously, Morley's introduction of Pêcheux's concept of 'interdiscourse', as far as it plays at the level of discourse only, was of no significance at all to the active audience he was searching for. We should carry this argument all the way through, and it is our basic point. But lucky as he was, Morley went beyond the limit of the pure discourse and regarded the 'interdiscourse' as Althusser's 'interpellation' that occurs concretely. He finds out two moments when, or two structures where, the 'interdiscourse' functions concretely: the 'constituted subjects' and the 'specific discursive positions'⁵⁹, or, 'the sub-

---

57 | Quoted in David Morley, *Television, Audiences and Cultural Studies*, p. 62. Morley does not indicate the source of this quotation, and standardised the originally italicised words, which is now corrected against Louis Althusser, *Positions [1964-1975]*, p. 110.
58 | Quoted in David Morley, *Television, Audiences and Cultural Studies*, p. 62. The original text of this quotation is 'il n'y a d'idéologie que pour des sujets concrets' (Althusser, *Positions [1964-1975]*, p. 110), which seems a bit stylistically weaker than its English rendition 'there is no ideology except for concrete subjects' that Morely used. To follow Morley's understanding, we did not translate it as 'there is no ideology but that for concrete subjects'.
59 | David Morley, *Television, Audiences and Cultural Studies*, p. 60.

ject in general' and 'the discursive formation of specific societies'[60]. According to the psychoanalysis as far as he understood, the subject has been already constituted by the Oedipus complex, the mirror stage, the castration complex and its solution as revealed by psychoanalysis. This is a determined subject, so its reception of the text is determined accordingly: 'every specific reading is already determined by the primary structure of subject positions'[61]. But when the latter gets involved in the process, 'these interpellations are not given and absolute but, rather, are conditional and provisional, in so far as the struggle in ideology takes place precisely through the articulation/disarticulation of interpellation.'[62] In the dynamics of 'interdiscourse', 'The two structures involved (constitution of the subject/interpellation into specific discursive positions) are articulated, but are not identical,' reminded Morley, 'not mere replication of each other.'[63]

Similarly, what made Morley appreciate Laclau was that when Laclau borrowed Althusser's concept of 'interpellation', he did not swallow it whole, i.e., together with its attached psychoanalytical determinism, but cautiously and wittily placed it 'at the level of the play in and struggle over discourses' as quoted previously; and in so doing, the 'interpellation' would become dynamic and yield unlimited and unpredictable results. Needless to say, when turning to the dynamic interpellation, Morley was definitely not so simple-minded as to have neglected the 'dominant decoding' as Hall proposed, or, to have cancelled the pre-determined subjects of psychoanalysis, but revisited and re-interpreted them in terms of his favoured 'discursive space', or, 'interdiscursive space'. This is a space that is full of the negotiations, contestations and oppositions among various discourses. Once the ideologically-constituted subject or the *dominant ideology* enters such a space, a magic space, they will be deprived of their privileged power: the subject will no longer be superior to the object,

---

60 | Ibid.
61 | Ibid.
62 | Ibid.
63 | Ibid., p. 62.

and the ideology will no longer retain its dominance over other discourses; they are, but, debased as one subject—to be precise, one individual—and one discourse, negotiating and competing with other subjects and discourses. Therefore, as Morley assumed, 'A successfully achieved correspondence [between the text and the reader] must be understood as *an accomplishment*, not *a given*. It is the result of an articulation; [...] but not of 'determination.'[64] In a particular reading, there is nothing that can be guaranteed and pre-determined. Whichever discourse it may be, so long as it persists and means to win, it must get involved in the struggle with other discourses. The negotiated or oppositional decoding is the result of this discourse struggle. The dominant decoding is of no exception. Their differences only appear in the *results*, i.e., what they are *finally; but in the process, they are all trying with every endeavour and providence to decode, articulate and disarticulate*. Decoding is intrinsically to strive, to overcome, in order for 'an accomplishment' as Morley observed!

Another point we'd like to add in passing is: when Morley took the 'interpellation' for the 'interdiscourse,' the 'interpellation' was no longer the one-way 'interpellation' to the concrete individual made by the determining ideology in the Althusserian sense, and no longer the pre-appointment of the linguistic, or symbolic, or Other's, unconscious with the subject in the Lacanian sense, which means that the subject is either linguistic, or symbolic, or the Other and has no other choices. It can be anything but in itself. As Lacan, among others, asserted, it does not speak but is spoken. The spoken subject or subjects are, as Morely precisely termed, the 'subjects-for-language'[65], who have been inscribed into or by the language. But, Morley's 'interpellation' was the interpellation of 'interdiscourse', and of discourses, in which the original meaning of the 'interpellation' that had been neglected by Althusser and Lacan was finally restored: *inter*-pellation, *inter-appellation*, i.e., appealing each other. The inter-ness presumed the fragmentation, shortage, incompleteness

---

64 | Ibid., p. 67. Emphasis added.
65 | Ibid., p. 61.

and insufficiency of each party involved in the 'interdiscourse' or 'interpellation' which aims, in turn, to cover the entire ground and the whole reality by endlessly weaving and scrapping, reweaving and re-scrapping the net of discourses. Where there are discourses, there are cracks; put another way, when discourses encounter with each other, there will arise cracks. But the cracks do not belong to the discourses themselves; or rather, they exist in between discourses and their realities. Being too much immersed in the discursive *cracks* as shown in, for instance, Pêcheux's 'interdiscourse', and Laclau's ideological 'interpellation' which is defined by the 'play' and 'struggle', Morley seemed to hold that the conception of the active audience can be obtained exclusively at the level of discourses if one sees a variety of discourses and their manifoldness and interactions. This was an inescapable misunderstanding that resulted from the discourse-centrism Morley had learned from Hall. There was no possibility for Hall to correct this misunderstanding, because it was just from the discourse-centrism that he found faults with personal and private readings. Morley had a chance to clear away this misunderstanding when he criticised the Althusserian theory of the discursive formation of subject, but he did not do the same to Hall who shared the discourse-centrism with Althusser; he gave up the chance anyhow. This suggests at least that Morely did not take seriously the discourse-centrism. No such centrism in his eye! It is noticed that Morley did not leave the discourse and enter the reality behind the discourse; rather, he held the discourse and danced with reality. Tracking historically, the way in which Morley did was the surviving influence of the structuralist theory of discourse for which, the text has nothing to do with the reality, as a radical dictum goes: '*Il n'y pas de hors-texte.*'[66] There is nothing outside the text: since all the reality has been *textualised*, *sign*ified, and transformed into the text, no reality can be found outside the text. Therefore, it is no wonder at all that one of Morley's trajectories, clear or not, is always from the discourse to the reality, looking at the reality from the discourse. For

---

66 | Jacques Derrida, *De la grammatologie*, Paris: Minuit, 1967, p. 227.

Morley, the discourse is primary, while the reality secondary; the discourse original, and the reality a copy of it. There is no reality of its own, and all the reality is in discourse and then discursive. To extend this, all individuals are *subjects*, or, *effects* of discourses. Thus this is to say, the difference between Morley and the psychoanalysis he criticised lies only in that: psychoanalysis just believes in one single discourse, i.e., the 'primary and universal'[67] discourse, which has been internalised into the 'psychoanalytic processes'[68], while Morley interpreted the discourse as multi-folded discourse, or, *inter*-discourse, which is in the *inter*-pellation. This seems to suggest that it is still within the scope of discourse that Morley could turn a monistic determinism into an 'over-determination'. As clearly asserted above, the multi-discourse determination of the subject is actually no determination of any single discourse. It is only by means of interacting with other discourses that a discursive subject can be attained. Thus, the audience will become an undetermined 'subject' or a discursive effect. But the fact is, neither Freud's nor Lacan's psychoanalysis, nor Althusser's ideological theory, is a monistic determinism, if we can call either of them determinism, as besides language, discourse or ideology, Freud has the *instinct*, Lacan the *réel*, and Althusser the *economic base*, to engage the determination. The problem they have in common, however, lies in their inability or failure to articulate and integrate the discourse and the reality: they are often trapped in the theoretical dilemma of caring for one while neglecting the other and the one-sided readings caused by such a dilemma. This tends to incur a misreading of them. Has Lacan ever taken the unconscious exclusively as the linguistic *Autre* and thus betrayed Freud who treats the unconscious as the *instinct*? Conversely speaking, how could Freud only fill his 'instinct' into the unconscious while refusing any culture or civilization to enter it? No, they are misrepresented! Lacan and Althusser are not the men of *letters* that exclude all realities, while Freud not the man of *distinct* that refuses to be put into letters!

---

67 | David Morley, *Television, Audiences and Cultural Studies*, p. 59.
68 | Ibid.

Mencius, a Chinese ancient sage, warns us: 'Believing in books is no better than having no books!' He has in mind both books and realities.

Morley understood Freud one-sidedly, if not wrongly. He only knew a Lacanised—linguistic—Freud, though the linguistic unconscious is part of the Freudian psychoanalysis. He only knew a Freud holding the determinism of the linguistic unconscious, but did not know there was also a Freud with the 'instinct' unconscious. It is thus seen that in his passage about Althusser who left aside Freud's unconscious, Morley regarded Freud's unconscious as the Lacanian language, and further, as the determinism for the subject, by which there will be only a passive audience. He did not know at all that it was just Freud's 'instinct' that could finally—after all other means had been tried but failed—assure the active audience he desperately needed. The 'instinct' will not make the subject passive; on the contrary, only 'instinct' can remind us finally of the imaginariness of the ideological discourses, the deception of the 'cultural industry,' and the heterogeneity of 'cultural imperialism', etc. He criticised Freud, Lacan and Althusser from the perspective of language or discourse, while, as what has been illustrated above, he also attempted to seek cracks or breakthroughs between discourses, i.e., in the *discursive space* or *interdiscursive space*. In such a discursive way, Morley believed, the discursive control of the psychoanalysis of his interpretation could be loosened or broken. It may be helpful to use a discursive way to deconstruct a discursive dominance, but it is helpful only to certain extent. For a final active audience, the discursive way is *methodologically* wrong: as a Chinese saying goes, 'Climbing the tree to hunt the fish.' Indeed, a discursive way, or more subtle, an interdiscursive way, rather than a way between discourse and reality, would be just a waste of time for Morley himself; and what may be worse, for Freud, Lacan and Althusser, it would be a waste of sources: when he criticised their discourse-centrism, Morley should have exposed the reality that has been deeply buried in discourses, and he should have placed the discourse into its interaction with the reality, but he failed to do so—what a pity it was!

However, these technical—if not inconsiderable—mistakes did not frustrate Morley's conceptualisation of the active audience. We are much relieved to see that when he abandoned the external and redundant burdens of theory and proceeded with his own ethnographic studies of audiences, he not only achieved his active audience theory with ease, but also effortlessly got access to *psycho*analysis (Freud and Lacan) and *ideo*-analysis (Althusser)[69] which used to confuse and haunt him theoretically or philosophically. Was Althusser after all a determinist of ideology/discourse, or of economy? If the ideology/discourse determines the formation of the subject, just like what Lacan's linguistic unconscious does, can it then become a force to actively resist an alien discourse, for instance, 'cultural imperialism', in the context of globalisation? In what sense is the subject passive, or, active? In the Freudian doctrine, is there a space for the linguistic unconscious developed by Lacan? Was Lacan a Judas, as usually imagined, to Freud in his linguistic interpretation of the unconscious? These questions have been touched upon more or less above, but which is definitely not enough, considering that they are complicated and significant. It is tempting to do a systematic and deep study into them, but to more concentrate on our present topic, we have to leave them aside. Now we would like to reiterate, without going into much details for the moment, that: the activeness of the audience is rooted in its *unconscious* or *instinct* which is the very base for its dialogue with the media discourse; and a discourse has to forgo or forget its discursiveness and dwell with the unconscious, which is to say, to become the unconscious discourse, or, the ontological discourse, before it can become a force of resistance. Morley did not make so clear an assertion like this, but his ethnographic studies of audiences and the explanation thereto, as I read them, have indicated this without any reservation. It is implied that: in Morley's wandering definition of the audience, no matter as subjects/discourses, or, as the unconscious/

---

69 | The term 'ideo-analysis' is coined here to show the similarity between Freud-Lacan's *psycho*analysis and Althusser's *ideo*logical analysis.

instinct, he always struggled for a concept of the *socio-ontological* audience, although staggering all the way, but never gave up.

Chapter Three.
Towards a New Materialistic Conception of Audiences

Morley would certainly not admit the audience as the Freudian *instinct*, and his ontology of the audience almost had nothing to do with psychology, let alone biology or physiology. The philosophical perspective that he intended to develop was 'socio-ontology', according to which the audience are individuals who are living in a given society.

Morley mentioned V. N. Vološinov's concept of 'social individual' more than once, but it is a pity that he had never given a detailed and significant explanation to it.[1] However, from my point of view,

---

1 | David Morley, *Television, Audiences and Cultural Studies*, p. 282. As a matter of fact, there is no such term, *to the letter*, as 'social individual', quoted by Morley, in V. N. Vološinov's *Marxism and Philosophy of Language*; however, there does be a thematic topic of 'social individual' throughout the book. For Vološinov, the 'social' is a defining characteristic of the individual that is socially formed, and there is no individual without social dimension. Vološinov distinguished between the 'natural individual' and if it may exist *literally*, the 'social individual': 'To avoid misunderstandings, a rigorous distinction must always be made between the concept of the individual as natural specimen without reference to the social world (i.e., the individual as object of the biologist's knowledge and study) and the concept of individuality which has the status of an ideological-semiotic superstructure over the natural individual and which, therefore, is *a social concept* [emphasis added]. These two meanings of the word "individual" (the

his entire studies of the audience, ethnographic and theoretical, was trying to explain how the audience is social individuals, and why it contains the force of resistance because of its being socially individual. If purely as a social structure, the audience may have no direct

natural specimen and the person) are commonly confused, with the result that the arguments of most philosophers and psychologists constantly exhibit *quaternio terminorum*: now one concept is in force, now the other takes its place.' (V. N. Vološinov, *Marxism and Philosophy of Language*, trans. Ladislav Matejka and I. R. Titunik, Cambridge, Massachusetts & London: Harvard University Press, 1986, p. 34) Obviously Vološinov determined, with the distinction he made, to choose the social dimension of individuals while excluding the natural one; or rather, only a concept of 'social individual' can be adopted for him. But in the meanwhile, he did not deny at all the fact that there is a concept of 'natural individual', and further there is a natural foundation for every individual, and a material foundation for a society. Because of his over-emphasis upon the social and ideological 'superstructure' of individuals, he did not make a substantial contribution to the resolution of a more complex problem of how the social and the natural are interrelated with each other. The same problem occurred with Althusser of the 1970's, by whom the *linguistic*—if not *ideological*—Lacan was foregrounded, while the Lacan of the *réel* was ignored. To establish his or her individuality, one has to be associated with and also differentiated from others, but which does not mean that by the association and differentiation he or she will be totally transformed or dispersed into others, into ideology, or into the social.

When importing the 'social individual' into his active audience theory, Morley just found a *social* individual, while a *natural* individual was overlooked. An evidence of this can be seen from that in his *The 'Nationwide' Audience* Morley contrasted the social of individuals in Vološinov sharply against the private of individuals in the 'uses and gratifications' model, with an aim to integrate them (see David Morley, *The 'Nationwide' Audience: Structure and Decoding*, pp. 14-15), which is to say, he did not realise that for Vološinov there is indeed a natural dimension of individuals. Differently from, if not quite contrarily to, Morley, as seen in the text that follows, we will give

relationship with Freud's 'instinct'; but if speaking of the audience as individuals, no matter social or not, and inquiring further what else an individual will be besides being a social structure, Morley should have thought over Freud's 'instinct', at least taking it as one of his theoretical sources. A passage through which he blundered to Freud is, among others, the *'uses and gratifications'* model, which, as an audience-centred model, has been well received and practiced by many till now. This model is aimed, according to a widely-taught textbook, at a shift from studying 'what the media do with people' to studying 'what people do with the media'; it looks at how audiences use the media contents and how they get gratifications from the use; thus, it holds: 'Audience behaviour [sic] is to a large extent to be explained by the *needs* and *interests* of the individual.'[2] Morley was very familiar with this model, and as early as in 1974, in his 'Reconceptualising the Media Audience: Towards an Ethnography of Audiences', a working paper yet a manifesto of his audience studies, Morley sifted it out as a rival, which is contesting yet allied with his own model of the active audience. They were both emphasising the audience's active interpretations of the media contents, and the shift from contents to audiences as indicated above, by which an audience study, of whatever kind, can be made possible. But in explaining why the audience is active, they were *fundamentally* different for Morley, nonetheless:

We need to break fundamentally with the 'uses and gratifications' approach, with its psychologistic problematic and its emphasis on *individual* differences of interpretation. Of course, there will always be individual 'private' readings; but we need to see the way in which these readings are patterned into cultural structures and clusters. What is needed here is an

---

prominence to the natural dimension of individuals that should be liberated from the suppression made by Vološinov and Althusser as well. What Morley did with the 'social individual' may be nothing but to put Vološinov in the ideological framework of Althusser.

2 | Dennis McQuail & Sven Windahl, *Communication Models for the Study of Mass Communications*, London & New York: Longman, 1981, p. 75.

approach which links differential interpretations back to the socio-economic structure of society—showing how members of different groups and classes, sharing different 'cultural codes' will interpret a given message differently, not just at the level of idiosyncratic personal differences of interpretation, but in a way systematically related to their socio-economic position.[3]

To put it simply, the difference between the two approaches is that: one accentuates the individuality of audiences while the other takes their sociality as a more important factor. This recognition and assessment of the 'uses and gratifications' approach repeatedly appeared in Morley's later accounts of the active audience: for example, the above quotation was included into his book *Television, Audiences and Cultural Studies*, almost to the letter. The repetition of this kind was made more than once.[4] As he identified, the individuality in the 'uses and gratifications' approach has much to do with psychology; and this psychology is influenced by Freud's psychoanalysis vaguely and subtly. For instance, K. E. Rosengren's mode has referred to A. H. Maslow's hierarchy of needs which is not far from Freud's doctrine: 'With a reference to Maslow's (1954) hierarchy of needs,' as stated in a textbook, 'Rosengren claims that the higher level needs (the need for company, love, acceptance and self-actualization) are those of most relevance for the uses and gratifications models, compared to the lower level needs (psychological and safety needs).'[5] In fact, it is a common sense that 'a number of important communication theories in use today' which 'look inside the individual for the forces impelling behavior change' have scarcely evaded the impact generated by Freud, though they may not be properly categorised as

---

[3] | Dave Morley, 'Reconceptualising the Media Audience: Towards an Ethnography of Audiences', the University of Birmingham, CCCS Stenciled Occasional Paper, 1974, p. 1.
[4] | David Morley, *Television, Audiences and Cultural Studies*, p. 54, p. 88.
[5] | Dennis McQuail & Sven Windahl, *Communication Models for the Study of Mass Communications*, p. 76.

psychoanalysis, because 'psychoanalytic theory assumes that explanations of human behavior lay within the individual, and especially in the unconscious.'[6] Morley's audiences are certainly not individuals in the sense of psychoanalysis or broadly, psychology, but they are still individuals in some other sense; even if Morley attempted to deprive the individuals of the psychological contents and refill them with the sociological ones, but individuals are after all individuals: if the individual is not made of society, discourse and ideology alone, then it must be the individual that has a biological substratum on the other hand. If there is no purely biological individual, there will be no purely social individual either. An individual should be both sociological and biological. This is the reason why the communication studies of the 20th century accepted Freud's psychoanalysis, which is 'individualistic, looking within the individual, especially the individual's childhood experiences, buried in the unconscious, for explanations of behavior'[7], besides Darwin's evolutionary theory and Marx's historical materialism, each of which works 'at the macro level of society'[8]. After Freud, who dares to talk about an individual with no body but spirit only? To be exact, what Morley intended to demarcate was not the audience as individuals but as *psychological* individuals as claimed by the 'uses and gratifications' approach, despite the fact that no one, Morley included, has ever accomplished this. Morley's active audience included an individual that had been updated socially. Without individuality, there is no active audience, no matter how this individuality is reshaped or theoretically revised.

The *individuality* is the starting point—if not only—for Morley to re-conceptualise the media audience in his early years, and is the

---

6 | Everett. M. Rogers, *A History of Communication Study: A Biographical Approach*, New York: The Free Press, 1997 [1994], p. 86. According to Rogers, Darwin, Freud and Marx are the three major influences from the 19th century Europe on the social sciences including communication studies in America since 1900 (See ibid., p. 34 and p. 86).
7 | Ibid.
8 | Ibid.

logical premise of his ethnographic studies of audiences as well. Although he disparaged the *psychological* individual of the 'uses and gratifications' model and intended to replace it with the 'social individual', he still praised it in this way: 'This approach highlights the important fact that *different members* of the media audience may "use" and interpret any particular programme in a quite different way from how the communicator intended it, and in quite different ways from *other members* of the audience.'[9] This suggests that Morley bathed the 'uses and gratifications' but did not throw the 'baby' out with the bath water: he liberated the word, *audience*, from its constraint of being a collective noun, and regarded it plural, i.e., the audience *are* 'different members' of the people. This can certainly be understood as individualising or *singularising* the audience. In the same paper as quoted above, he also warned: 'We must not see the audience as an undifferentiated mass'[10]. As easily discerned, it is the *undifferentiated audience* supposed by the Frankfurt School that leaves no space for the audience, in the sense of which the audience is the passive receiver of messages, the innocent profit-realiser of the capitalist 'culture industry', and therefore, no significance, though necessary, to the communication circuit. Morley should have deeply known that to break through the pessimistic assumption of 'culture industry', he had to strategically demassify and divide the *audience* into concrete individuals. Although, as it is noticeable on the other side, Morley loved to take his *demassified*—as we have just suggested—audience as 'overlapping subgroups, each with its own history and cultural traditions'[11], such 'subgroups', from which he identified a different response to the encoded messages that the communicators intend, would be reasonably for him made of various individuals, since if he does not want to restore these groups as the *masses* as the Frankfurt School assumed, then he would have to prove or admit that these

---

9 | Dave Morley, 'Reconceptualising the Media Audience: Towards an Ethnography of Audiences', p. 1. Emphasis added.
10 | Ibid., p. 8.
11 | Ibid.

groups consist of individuals. They are groups of *individuals*, or, they are *individuals* in the form of group! Whether or not a group or a community can be formed and well grow will mainly depend on if it is essentially related to and can protect the real interests of its individuals. Its 'history' as a 'cultural tradition', however, may disguise the real interests of its individuals or any other kinds of material foundation. According to Benedict Anderson's famous saying of nation, any group should be an *imagined* group, *articulated* by *discourse*. True as this may be, we would still like to say further that: on the counter sides of the imaginations or discourses there is the engraved truth of each individual that is hard for us to erase.

Morley did not give a detailed explanation to the 'social individual', a term unauthorised by Vološinov as the previous textual research has proved, but he did elucidate the 'social individual' generally, anyhow. A brief description, if not as a strict definition, was given by Morley, though indirectly: the so called 'social individual' is, as far as it is in the process of communication, 'the individual decoder in a given structured social context'[12]. This quasi-definition clearly indicates two dimensions of the interaction in a decoder: first, the 'individual, varied, experience and response', and second, the other 'the cultural resources available' 'in a particular social context'.[13] Morley did not validate the arbitrariness of individual reading, nor did he approve the social or cultural determinism. Instead, he placed the 'individual' into its dynamic relationship with 'society'. In most cases, as already known to us, Morley viewed 'society' as constructed by discourses from a structural perspective; but, from time to time, he sociologically represented it as age, gender, race, class, etc., and even employed, albeit occasionally, such terms like 'socio-economic structure' or 'socio-economic position'[14], which suggests that he had semantically laid the *society* on a par with the *economy* and intended a material, for instance, economic, existence of the society. Although, for Morley,

---

12 | David Morley, *Television, Audiences and Cultural Studies*, p. 90.
13 | Ibid.
14 | Ibid., p. 88.

the individual has never existed purely as individual but always as a discursive or interdiscursive individual, when he was opposed to replacing 'the category of individual—as actor in a social world'—with 'the category of social class', and opposed to reducing an individual to the 'social class he or she belonged to', [15]what else then would be this *individual* that has refused all the appointments from outside and isolated himself or herself from the 'society' and 'class' of which he or she is actually a member? Whether or not he had realised all the time, Morley in fact kept drawing us to the origin of 'individual' that had been denied by Hall as a 'private'—or, the alternative words Morley chose for which were 'psychological', 'idiosyncratic', and 'personal'—'matter' which was mixed by Morley with the 'cultural structures and clusters'. The individual in the place of its origin, or, to be brief, the original individual, may not be properly described as Freud's 'instinct', but it is unfailingly something not far from the 'instinct'. It is not deathly needed for us to insist upon describing the nature of the individual, apart from its social formations, as 'instinct', but we must acknowledge that it is the human bodily existence that underpins and interacts with the social properties. No doubt, as Marx taught, 'the essence of man [...] is the ensemble of the social relations'[16], but the 'essence' and 'social relations', both of which are abstract at different levels (the former is philosophically abstract; and the latter sociologically abstract), need to physically dwell in a place such as flesh and blood, productive forces, economic base, everyday life, etc., otherwise man of that 'essence' or those 'social relations' will be no longer the 'man' in the world, but purely intellectual, spiritual, or, just as the ideological subject.

Morley apparently did not welcome such a purely intellectual, spiritual or ideological audience. In a response to the skepticism about the empirical research on audiences, Morley critically analysed the argument put forward by, among others, John Hartley and John Fis-

---

15 | Ibid., p. 89.
16 | Karl Marx, 'Theses on Feuerbach', in David McLellan (ed.), *Karl Marx: Selected Writings*, Oxford: Oxford University Press, 1977, p. 157.

ke, that the audience is constructed exclusively by discourses beyond which there is no audience at all. This argument looks quite Lacanian or Althusserian! As an Althusserian on the one hand but Lacanian on the other hand, Morley made a dialectical conceptualisation of the audience:

it is possible to recognize the necessarily constructivist dimension of any research process without claiming that audiences only *exist* discursively. To argue otherwise is to confuse a problem of epistemology with one of ontology. Naturally, any empirical knowledge which we may generate of television audiences will be constructed through particular discursive practices, and the categories and questions present and absent in those discourses will determine the nature of the knowledge we can generate. However, this is to argue, contra Hartley, that while we can only know audiences through discourses, audiences do in fact exist outside the terms of these discourses.[17]

And as to the *society*, he once again expressed his dialectics, by quoting C. Gledhill:

Under the insistence of the semiotic production of meaning, the effectivity of social, economic and political practice threatens to disappear altogether. There is a danger of conflating the social structure of reality with its signification, by virtue of the fact that social processes and relations have to be mediated through language, and the evidence that the mediating power of language reflects back on the social process. But to say that language has a determining effect on society is a different matter from saying that society is nothing but its languages and signifying practices.[18]

Morley had thought highly of the discursive and ideological dimension of the *individual* and *society*, as we know it, yet when he had to

---

17 | David Morley, *Television, Audiences and Cultural Studies*, p. 178.
18 | Quoted in David Morley, *Television, Audiences and Cultural Studies*, pp. 178-179.

defend his empirical studies of audiences, he resolutely turned himself to ontologically affirm the existence of the individual and society. It is no mistake to look at the individual and society *epistemologically*, but an epistemological view of them will be no mistake either. Anything in the world of man is both in itself and for man, which conceptually does not involve any contradictions. Perhaps a passage Morley quoted from E. H. Carr may be extended as an emphasis on the distinction, or a clarification of the intriguing relationship, between the thing *in* discourse and that *outside* discourse:

> It does not follow that, because a mountain appears to take on different shapes from different angles of vision, it has objectively either no shape at all or an infinity of shapes. It does not follow that because interpretation plays a necessary part in establishing the facts of history, and because no existing interpretation is wholly objective, that one interpretation is as good as another.[19]

Morely did not lapse into Nietzsche's perspectivism and the poetic narratology of the American New Historicism (in Hayden White, for example), but believed in the *facticity* in interpretations, the *historicity* in narrations, the *truthfulness* in representation, and therefore the *audience-beyond-discourses*, even though which he had not fully clarified. He would certainly not consider such an audience a physical existence or 'instinct', but as for the non-discursive existence of the social, the individual, or, the social individual, he seemed to take delight in calling it 'material existence', which may be seen from his exposition and criticism, through Iain Chambers, of the linguistic self-imprisonment of structuralism and semiotics:

> by putting between brackets, or simply failing to acknowledge, the *material conditions* of the practices they examine, and treating them and so-

---

19 | Quoted in David Morley, *Television, Audiences and Cultural Studies*, p. 179.

ciety solely as a sign system, structuralism and semiotics have remained caught in the very ideology they claim to have exposed.[20]

And Morley continues to search for support from Chambers:

Codes, like ideas, do not drop from the skies, they arise within the *material practices* of production. However, Barthes reduces that production to a single moment in the process: the Text; and turns that moment into a self-reflexive totality divorced from its *material existence*.[21]

About these two passages of Chambers, Morley made almost no comments after quoting them. This is certainly consistent with Morley's writing style, but the more essential reason is actually that these statements are too clear, too thorough, and too penetrating for Morley to shoot off his mouth. And what's more, Morley had made some explanations to the similar quotes just before introducing Chambers:

We cannot study language simply as a closed system, a technical instrument of communication: it is inevitably situated in the whole field of socio-political relations within which communication occurs. It was from this perspective that Iain Chambers criticized Barthes and his more formalist disciples [...][22]

Morley shared in Chamber's criticism of structuralism and semiotics. Although only Barthes was mentioned here by Chambers and Morley, their criticism could be also extended to Lacan and Althusser who were Barthes' more formalist *colleagues* if not *disciples*; or, perhaps, even to Hall whose model implied a *discourse-centrism*. If this was the case, then the criticism could be read as the clarification and

---

20 | Quoted in David Morley, *Television, Audiences and Cultural Studies*, p. 33. Emphasis added.
21 | Quoted in David Morley, *Television, Audiences and Cultural Studies*, p. 33. Emphasis added.
22 | David Morley, *Television, Audiences and Cultural Studies*, p. 33.

therefore re-adjustment of Morley's own thought on the relationship between the audience and discourse: from now on, the audience for Morley will be both within discourse and beyond discourse; and there is always a dialogue between the discourse in itself and the discourse for us. As for the 'audience' beyond discourse, Morley was trying to understand it from the perspective of 'social individual'. Although he could not regard the audience-beyond-discourse an instinctive existence, the concept 'material existence' that he had quoted from Chambers was actually synonymous with the instinctive existence of the individual. This 'material existence', as suggested by the above quotations, belongs to the 'individual' which, however, is defined by structuralists with sign, discourse, ideology and text—say, which was ideologically abstracted as 'subject' by Althusser. As is known to many, the core argument of structuralism or postmodernism, broadly, is the death of subject; but, as is known to few, the death of subject implies simultaneously the revival of individual, otherness, strangeness, esotericality, singularity, or, irrationality if you like. Considering this, postmodernism should be the legitimate successor to the Romanticism of the 19th century's literature.

If the individual has a *material existence*, as Morley acknowledged it, through or with Chambers, his or her material existence should be for words a hard core, a Dark Continent, i.e., instinct or the unconscious, a psychoanalytic existence, or at a visible or social level, the material conditions or foundations for the everyday practice of the individual. To hold the former is Freudianism while the latter is Marxism. Terry Eagleton perceived the similarity between the two theories. He discovered that as an instinct-believer on the one hand, Freud, on the other hand, spoke out a fundamental tenet of Marxism as well: 'The motive of human society is in the last resort an economic one.'[23] In response to the accusation made by the political

---

23 | Terry Eagleton, *Literary Theory: An Introduction*, 2nd ed., Minneapolis: The University of Minnesota Press, 1996, p. 131. In a subsequent text Eagleton once again referred to this Marxist thesis made by Freud: 'all societies, Freud comments in Marxian vein, have at root an economic motive.'

Left of Freud who 'substitutes "private" psychological causes and explanations for social and historical ones', Eagleton refuted that 'This accusation reflects a radical misunderstanding of Freudian theory', and contended: 'What Freud produces, indeed, is nothing less than a materialist theory of the making of the human subject.' Of course, Eagleton still had to admit that 'There is indeed a real problem about how social and historical factors are *related* to the unconscious',[24] and perhaps this 'problem' may be converted into our question: How

---

(Terry Eagleton, *The Ideology of the Aesthetic*, Oxford: Basil Blackwell, 1990, p. 276. It was indicated by Eagleton that Freud had this comment in his *A General Introduction to Psychoanalysis*, New York, 1943, p. 273)

24 | Terry Eagleton, *Literary Theory: An Introduction*, p. 141. Eagleton not only recognised Freud in Marx, but also Marx in Freud, which was illustrated especially in his book *The Ideology of the Aesthetic*: by means of the *aesthetic* and *body*, both of which are characteristically relating to sense and perception, he connected Marx with Freud as well as Nietzsche, indicating that: 'there might, nevertheless, be some way of working laboriously upwards from the opposing thumb or the oral drive to mystical ecstasy and the military-industrial complex. And it is just this kind of project which the three greatest "aestheticians" of the modern period—Marx, Nietzsche and Freud—will courageously launch: Marx with the labouring body, Nietzsche with the body as power, Freud with the body of desire' (Terry Eagleton, *The Ideology of the Aesthetic*, p. 197). If this is still not as clear as needed, then a clearer case will be that when making reference to other scholars' achievements, Eagleton straightforwardly equated body with economy: 'The system of economic production, as [Elaine] Scarry points out, is for Marx a kind of materialized metaphor of the body, as when he speaks in the *Grundrisse* of agriculture as a conversion of the soil into the body's prolongation. Capital acts as the capitalist's surrogate body, providing him with a vicarious form of sentience; and if the ghostly essence of objects is exchange-value, then it is their material use-value, as Marx again comments in the *Grundrisse*, which endows them with corporeal existence.' (Ibid., p. 198) In this sense, Eagleton perhaps should not oppose to such argument we would like to develop: the 'material existence' of individuals

could one reasonably associate the *material existence* of the individual's psychology, i.e., the instinct, with his or her social *material existence*, say, the economic base? It can be thought that Morley's redefinition of the audience with 'social individual' would be a good solution to this problem; this is to say, Morley had set up a *social ontology of the audience*, although, as it appeared, he himself did not put much emphasis on 'social individual', and did not propose to place 'audience' into the social ontology. Actually it was not Morley alone but together with us who constructed the social ontology of the audience. We will not deny our participation in this ontological construction, but nevertheless, what role we have played is just to objectively present what he really thought but did noAs we admit it, Morley would not deem the *social individual*, if separately speaking, either the *social* or the *individual*, just as a material existence; Rather, he would like to regard it *intellectual* or *spiritual*, and would like to reveal how they are, by ideologies and discourses, colonised and structuralised, and how, if in an Althusserian note, the *individual* is *interpellated* by the *social* into a *social subject*. However, what distinguished Morley from others was not that, as exposed previously, he held a comprehensive and therefore dialectic view of the audience, simultaneously placing the audience within and beyond discourses, but that, as Heidegger and Gadamer did in their philosophy and hermeneutics, *he treated the epistemology of the audience ontologically*. As far as his direct source is concerned, Morley might have been infiltrated by, among many, Williams' definition of culture which included the whole life, not only of the intellectual, the spiritual, but also the material, and which was *a way of life*, to be concise. This definition took culture as life, thereby bringing culture back to its origin, to the earth, as represented in such terms like 'agriculture' and 'horticulture', and to everyday life. Thus, this view of culture may be properly called as a 'life-ontology of culture'. Morley did not go far, as he just revised Williams' 'life' and made it his own 'society', which should be

---

is comprised not only of the instinct and desire of body, but also of the social material practices with which body matters.

no violence upon Williams, because the 'life' in William's definition of culture was never the life in itself but the 'way of life', and a life in a *way* is no difference with that in a *society* by which life is directed to and organised as *society*. If a life refrains itself from entering a society, it will not be the life that has a way. It is the society that gives the life a way. Such a way is a way-in/out, a start, a move forward, and it is a linguistic act, 'le Nom du Père', an ideology, a social norm, and furthermore, it is a signifying system or a God by which we can survive through any hardships of life, and it is also a cultural tradition some of us always want to break *through* but only to break *inside*. When their life turns into a way of life, people have been civilised, living in a social system which, however, tends to get caught in a paradox of two extremes: when you have it, you feel a burden in need of laying it down, but when we lose it, you feel a void in need of filling it up. The 'way of life' for Williams was only another expression for the 'society'; therefore, to say culture is a way of life will be the same as to say *culture is society*. After Williams, we would perhaps no longer think of culture as *intellectual* and *spiritual* while society *institutional* and *material*: culture and/as society are both abstract and concrete.

Following Williams' cultural materialism to move forward, but differing from such a route, Morley, in his social ontology of the audience, neither established his audience on the individual's material existence, nor did he believe in its spiritual existence; rather, he placed the audience in society, that is, in *everyday life*. From R. Silverstone, he quoted: 'Television is everyday life.'[25] According to Silverstone, with whom Morley identified, television studies had traditionally overlooked how television was integrated into or actively engaged in the daily life of the audience[26]. Morley supported an argument made by J. A. Radway that: 'we need to investigate the ways in which a whole variety of media is enmeshed in the production of popular

---

25 | Quoted in David Morley, *Television, Audiences and Cultural Studies*, p. 197.
26 | See David Morley, *Television, Audiences and Cultural Studies*, p. 197.

culture and consciousness across *the terrain of everyday life*'²⁷, which 'is to argue that the focus on the embedded audience must certainly now be a priority for media research.'²⁸ The so-called 'the embedded audience' here is the audience that is embedded, to be detailed, in its *everyday life*.

And for Morey's audience studies, for example, his *Family Television*, the everyday life where the audience is embedded is 'the domestic context'²⁹ in particular. Morley's trajectory from *society* to *everyday life*, and then to *domestic context*, albeit more and more down to earth, may on the other hand run the risk of being belittled as more and more narrowed and then trifling. In fact, Morley knew that he was accused of getting away from the right track of communications and cultural studies, of not caring about the questions of ideology or pubic issues but, taking a 'retreat into the sitting room', by which his political edge was blunted then.³⁰ Against this criticism, Morley had a forceful self-defence, which reads: the most natural place for people to most frequently watch TV is domestic, and although TV may be watched everywhere with the development of technologies, 'the problem is that viewing television is done quite differently in the home as opposed to in public places'³¹. Morley's defence involved two theoretical premises for the viewing or decoding of television: first, the context of viewing is quite determining to the viewing or decoding; at least, as Morley suggested, 'it is necessary to consider the *context of viewing* as much as the *object of viewing*'³². Second, this context of viewing should not be regarded as a *con*-text but part of the text,

---

27 | David Morley, *Television, Audiences and Cultural Studies*, p. 195. Emphasis added. This quotation is Morley's restatement of Radway's argument.
28 | Ibid., pp. 196-197.
29 | Ibid., p. 184.
30 | See David Morley, *Television, Audiences and Cultural Studies*, p. 168.
31 | David Morley, *Television, Audiences and Cultural Studies*, p. 133.
32 | Ibid., p. 157.

i.e., the text *itself*; it is an organic part of the viewing act[33]. Needless to add, this viewing context is the daily life of the audience. Morley criticised the traditional film studies for its equating the film with its text while excluding the watching context from that film. Distancing himself from this approach, Morley defined film-watching as 'going to the pictures' or 'cinema-going'. With some mysterious colors, he began to draw: 'There is going out at night and the sense of relaxation combined with the sense of fun and excitement', and to make his drawing of cinema-going more vivid and impressive, he added by quoting: 'the queue, the entrance stalls, the foyer, cash desk, stairs, corridor, entering the cinema, the gangway, the seats, the music, the lights fading, darkness, the screen, which begins to glow as the silk curtains are opening'. This is 'the phenomenology of the whole "moment" of going to the pictures'. He thereby argued that 'Rather than selling individual films, cinema is best understood as having sold a habit, or a certain type of socialised experience', and we would like to add, cinema has sold, to bring to mind Williams, *a way of life* as well. Morley urged that an analysis of film content/subject should include as its necessary object the viewing context in which the film is consumed and it should not pattern on 'the literary tradition in prioritising the status of the text itself abstracted from the viewing context'. The same is with television studies; or rather, television studies should have 'more' to say about the viewing context—emphasised by Morley: 'There is *more* to watching television than what is on the screen—and that 'more' is, centrally, the domestic context in which viewing is conducted.'[34] Morley's *Family Television* is the work of such

---

33 | Launching his *Family Television* project, Morley held a strong antagonism to the approach by which the domestic context was just thought as 'a pre-given "backdrop" to the activity' of television viewing. It was highly intended for Morley in the project to include the use of television into the interpretation of television materials (see David Morley, *Family Television: Cultural Power and Domestic Leisure*, p. 13).

34 | See David Morley, *Television, Audiences and Cultural Studies*, pp. 157-158.

a concern, i.e., putting the *domestic context* into television studies. He cited a lot of ethnographic cases to show the relevance and then significance of the *domestic context* to television decoding. As one may ask, will a context change the effect of text? Or put in another way, can a text present different meanings in different contexts? Morley did not exaggerate the role of context to the extent of changing the text itself, but to such a question, his response was affirmative in principle, since once a text is created, in terms of itself, no one can change it, as it is the 'thing in itself', but its *Wirkungen* (effects) or *Erscheinungen* (appearances), which are usually called 'meanings', may vary according to different readers and the readers in different environments. This is a truth revealed by the German reception-aesthetics, chiefly represented by Wolfgang Iser and Hans Robert Jauss, but now just a standing dish. However, if the context is specified domestically, as Morley did, we still cannot tell whether different home contexts will make difference substantial to a television text, though we have to admit the defining role a context plays to its text. For example, will the same viewer come up with a different decoding when viewing the same program in different contexts? To this question, Morley had his positive proofs, but one may have negative proofs on the other hand. Differences are always there, but not all of them will necessarily matter. Lying in bed to read a story, for example, is not so different a way from sitting at a desk over a cup of tea to appreciate it. To be frank, it is not so tempting for us as to pick fault with Morley at this concrete level. We are never tempted to do this way. Rather, we are trying to sympathetically understand Morley: no matter what a role the domestic context he chose will play in the process of decoding, big or small, that he dug and exposed this context, trivial it may look at one's first sight, did intensify the context and its decisive function on texts that may be treated in general. So long as a perspective from a big context is adopted, Morley's small context, the home context, would have its significance: it was a *micro*-form of contextualism, which was blended with, supported by, led to, or rather, linked by Morley himself in the very beginning, with a *macro*-contextualism. Using Chinese metaphors, Morley believed that the autumn could be known through a look at a leaf, or similarly, the whole leopard could be known through a look at its spot. As Morley claimed, his later family television studies did not throw aside the earlier analytical framework of class, race, education and ideology he constructed in the 'Nationwide' project, but attempted 'to investigate these sociological dimensions of household structure within that larger framework', for instance, 'to trace precisely *how* gender (or class or race) operate in specific contexts'.[35] This is, in Sean Cubitt's terminology, 'the politics of the living room'[36], which Morley was happy to quote. Small as a living room may be, it is connected to all the politics of the outside world. So to speak, Morley did not reject the traditional 'grand narrative', but put it into practice at the domestic level, thereby creating paradigmatically a micro-politics of television cultural studies.

Why did Morley bother to venture those 'seemingly less political, more domestic issues'[37]? Was it just for expanding the territory of cultural politics? Morley certainly had such an intention, or even an ambition. He kept telling us that his audience research 'work has also involved an attempt to reframe the study of ideology within the *broader* context of domestic communications'[38]; and also that 'I have attempted to frame the analysis below of Family Television and of the Household Uses of Information and Communication Technology within a *broader* framework of the role of various media in articulating the private and public spheres, which (hopefully) allows us to articulate these micro-analyses to *broader* perspectives on macro-social issues of politics, power and culture'[39]; and that, for one more example, in fightback against the criticism that his family television studies retreated into the living room and therefore its political edge was blunted, Morley scornfully thought it involving 'a *very restricted*

---

35 | David Morley, *Television, Audiences and Cultural Studies*, p. 169.
36 | Quoted in David Morley, *Television, Audiences and Cultural Studies*, p. 140.
37 | David Morley, *Television, Audiences and Cultural Studies*, p. 169.
38 | Ibid., p. 1. Emphasis added.
39 | Ibid., p. 40. Emphasis added.

conception of what "politics" is'[40]. Morley repeatedly used the word 'broader' in these professions, which apparently indicates that he intended to strongly suggest that the import of the domestic context into cultural studies would really expand the territory of the latter, and would also liberate the restrained and clichéd conception of 'politics'. Out of question, this is one of his contributions to British cultural studies. However, there may be a more important contribution than this but behind this if we would like to see his professions more deeply: it is just at a micro-level, i.e., the level of individuals, their daily life and material existence, that all the macro-politics where the ideology and its education are mostly concerned, may work on people decisively. Spirit, concept or theory cannot run by itself; they must be concretised, internalised, and materialised to realise itself. As for their structure, they are not pure but mixed with others. For example, even Hegel who firmly believed in the Absolute Spirit had to set two stages before it: the subjective spirit, which amounts to the personal, and the objective spirit, which means the social. And the two spirits in the earlier stages will be sublated but contained by the Absolute Spirit in its consummation of the highest stage. That is to say, the Absolute Spirit is absolutely not exclusive but inclusive of all the others, otherwise it will not deserve the title 'absolute'. Another case is in Althusser's proposition, as quoted in the previous chapter, that *'all ideology interpellates the concrete individuals [les individus concrets] into concrete subjects [sujets concrets]'*. Although the subject has become part or a puppet of the ideology, it remains 'concrete', preserving its life though in a suppressed way; this is to say, the subject always keeps being an individual on the other hand; Certainly, the subject is not an individual in its full sense, yet it is never independent of an individual, and of an individual's material existence. Contesting with the 'culture industry' theory, a central issue of Morley's audience studies was how to view the media message (normally regarded as discourse or ideology) works on the audience. Accordingly, when all the concepts are viewed in relation to reality, there will emerge two

---

40 | Ibid., p. 168. Emphasis added.

gateways, by which media messages do to the audience: One is concept, and the other is reality. On the side of the audience, as already known to us, firstly, it is knitted and constructed by discourse; but secondly, it is embedded in society, in everyday life, and in domestic context, etc. The audience is then loaded with both concept (we do not need here to distinguish among concept, discourse and ideology) and reality. Double-loaded as this, the audience also has two gateways in responding to media message: concept and reality. Media messages and the audience, or reversely, the audience and media messages, meet and interact on each other through concept and reality. In such meeting and interaction, there should be a case as Hall's model described of the media-codes to the audience-codes at a conceptual level, but which never means that it is solely at this conceptual level that media codes can actually change the codes and material existence of the audience. And to be strict, one code can never substantially change another code only by itself, since the code is always the code of something else which is interrelated with reality. 'The weapon of criticism cannot,' warned Marx, '[...] supplant the criticism of weapons; and material force must be overthrown by material force.'[41] He was talking about the necessity of the proletarian violent revolution; but his argument can be applied to all the material activities of reformation. The theory has the power to change the reality, but the exercising of such a power has to go through the material power. After Marx, the reason means nothing, if it is not materialised. In a similar vein, the media message means nothing to the audience if it does not work on its material existence.

It was just his realisation of this point that Morley placed the function of media messages on the audience at a micro-level, allowing media messages to speak not just to the audience's *discourse*, but also to its *socially materialistic existence*. And what responds to media messages is not just the audience as discourse, but also the audience as material force. Because the discourse cannot function

---

41 | Karl Marx, 'Towards a Critique of Hegel's *Philosophy of Right*: Introduction', in David McLellan (ed.), *Karl Marx: Selected Writings*, p. 157.

by itself on the audience, and it has to go through or heavily rely on material forces, then the activeness in which the audience responds to media messages, we may finally conclude, would exist within the dimension of the audience as material existence, notwithstanding its discursive dimension. If this is the case, then Morley's main contribution to British cultural studies would be not just having extended his political or ideological analysis and criticism to family and private domains, but in so doing, produced a concept of the audience whose activeness was ascribed to its material existence at last.

A further exposition of this audience concept is needed theoretically here: if the *imbedded audience* is considered ontological, it functions, it functions materially, or instinctively, or ontologically, then can it still function epistemologically? To answer this question, we must dissect the elements that structure the renewed concept of 'audience' and sort out the interrelationship between them.

To Morley, as we have already been informed, the first layer of the content of his 'audience' concept is the 'interdiscourse' he borrowed from Pêcheux; and the second one is: the audience as the individual, or as the individual's instinct, or to be broader, as the material existence. Morley easily accepted the audience as 'interdiscourse', but being deeply influenced by Hall and Althusser, he always hesitated to admit a material audience, though he never totally denied it. Now let's turn to the third layer if not logically contradicted with the previous two: the audience as the *context* in which it is set, or speaking reversely, which may be more accurate, the context constitutes the basic existence of the audience, or, the context is part of the audience. Put in the simplest way, audience is the context, or, the context is the audience.

Morley was certainly not the first to take the audience as its context or vice versa, but he had seamlessly inlaid this definition of the audience into the framework of his audience studies. A bridge to the new concept of the audience for Morley was Ien Ang, who suggested that 'an audience does not merely consist of the aggregate of viewers of a specific programme, it should also be conceived of as engaging in the practice of watching television as such [...] so decoding must be seen as embedded in a general practice of television viewing.'[42] Encouraged by Ang, among others, Morley no longer took the audience as the pure viewer, but regarded the television viewing as a practice in which television viewers became television practisers. For both Ang and Morley, the most theoretically significant may not be the audience embedded in its viewing practice, but a conceptual change that occurs to the audience after it is placed into its practice, which means the audience as the viewer has become the 'audience' as the practiser. The former concept of 'audience' was epistemological in that the audience and the programme watched are of the dichotomous relationship between subject and object. The audience situated in such a relationship is not so much a real knower but quite a purer knower, a function to know. To get close to the object, this kind of subject should be the purer the better, not to be contaminated by the worldliness, the habitus as well as any cultural heritages. But the latter concept of 'audience' is basically ontological. The audience in this sense is a know*er*, an individual of knowing, who has his or her own desire, everyday life, social relation, and cultural and historical structure, all of which are engaged in television watching. The audience *in practice* brings about the ontological audience, and it also brings about the audience *in action*. This is not a tautology, but needs to be explained in details.

Since any action occurs at a particular place and at a particular time, or in other words, in a certain context, it then can be said that the action should involve the context, or, the context has entered the action and become an important part of this action. Just as Aristotle observed in his *Poetics*, action *is* character, that is to say, a person shows his or her personality or character through the actions; and actively speaking, a person will accomplish himself or herself through the actions. Being applied to the audience, this proposition would claim: the audience's action of television watching, or the 'practice' as

---

42 | Quoted in David Morley, *Television, Audiences and Cultural Studies*, p. 184.

Ang termed, or the 'activity'[43] as Morley called, will constitute the very existence of the audience. And now that the audience is its action, and the action involves the context, the audience can be further thought of as the context. To repeat this deduction in a different way if needed, an audience is nothing but what he or she does, and what context he or she does in: both behaviorism and contextualism can illuminate what the audience is. Probably one may say that Morley prefers the contextualism to the behaviorism when he defines the audience. But for Morley, no action, no context: one cannot imagine a context without reference to an action. In fact, it is noticeable that Morley began with the audience's action, went through the context where the audience acts, and finally reached the very being of the audience, which was the logical route Morley followed to do his audience research.

Confucius seemed far less subtle and complicated than Morley who may have been over-complicated by our interpretations. He made no distinction among the following Chinese terms '*suo yi*', '*suo you*' and '*suo an*' and simply piled them all up so as to show how a man appears to us. These terms came from *The Analects*, which went: 'See whom a man contacts with (*suo yi*). Observe by what he is motivated (*suo you*). Examine with what he is at ease (*suo an*). How can a man hide from us?! How can a man hide from us?!'[44] Translating Confucius' words into the language of audience studies, we may say like this: Ah, audience, audience, if you allow us ethnographic scholars to learn about your daily life, daily activities, daily meditations, in a word, the context of your television watching, how can you hide from us? To repeat once more, it is the audience's context that *ex*-hibites and *con*-structs the audience. The teaching of Confucius suggested to us that: apart from being its context, audience cannot be anything else. There is no audience outside the context.

Perhaps there is a need for more explanations. Some annotators take '*suo yi*' as 'what a man does'; thus, it seems that the teaching of

---

43 | David Morley, *Television, Audiences and Cultural Studies*, p. 184.
44 | Quoted in Yang Bojun, *An Interpretive Translation of Confucius'* Analects, Beijing: Chinese Books Press, 1982, p. 16.

Confucius only centers around one's action, or only observes one's action, while excluding the examination of the context in which one's action is taken. But even if we abide by this annotation, we still cannot remove the way of how to get along with people from Confucius' art of viewing people or the category of people's *Erscheinung* (appearance and exhibition). This is because the *'ren'*, roughly translated as 'benevolence', the core value of Confucianism, teaches how to get along with others so as to become a saint. This refers to the overall action and therefore the way of doing; but from the concrete acts that Confucius loved to promote—serving the parents, serving the monarch, making friends, working for the government, loving others, etc.—we may conclude that even if Confucius' art of viewing a man has only one approach—observing one's action—the action he observed to test a man would still get involved with others, since any act needs an object as the target to act towards. Act is always cont*act*, and re*act*; it is a relation, a field of relations, and therefore a context if you like. Jürgen Habermas' term 'communicative action' (*Kommunikatives Handeln*) may be considered a condensed form of what Confucius thought about how to view a man: there is no act in *itself* but *each other*; the act is nothing else than communication, both acting on and acted by *other*s. In a similar vein, i.e., by *practice* or *activity*, Morley has brought the context into the structure of the audience. If regarding the media communication as a 'communicative act', then it will make no sense to distinguish the audience, its action, and its context, as they three are essentially the same. No act, no audience; the audience appears through its acts. And no context, no act; the context is the nature of act: since the act takes (a) *place* in the context, or, the act needs a space and occurs in the space, the context or the space is certainly part of that act. The context is the act! As shown already, there is no audience outside its context; now we may put it further that there is no act outside its context either. Then a trinity is formed of the audience, its action, and its context, which is broken apart by *a* Western epistemology, but re-articulated and re-constructed by Morley's social ontology. For Morley, a pure subject, or a subject as the pure knowing, i.e., the subject in an epistemological sense, rather than as a social individual, a real man or woman, is facing the danger of being undermined. We will be back to this point later.

It was impossible for Morley to know the quotation above from Confucius, let alone extend it to his audience observations. But fortunately, he found a valuable support from the Chinese philosophy of art which had the same view with Confucius. He got it through R. Silverstone, and Silverstone got it from another scholar. Morley requoted what Silverstone quoted in his manuscript as follows:

> To draw a carp, Chinese masters warn, it is not enough to know the animal's morphology, study its anatomy or understand the physiological functions of its existence. They tell us that it is also necessary to consider the reed against which the carp brushes each morning while seeking its nourishment, the oblong stone behind which it conceals itself, or the rippling of water when it springs toward the surface. These elements should in no way be treated as the fish's environment, the milieu in which it evolves or the natural background against which it can be drawn. *They belong to the carp itself* [...] The carp must be apprehended as a certain power to affect and be affected by the world.[45]

Morley made his comments on this: 'It is in this connection that Silverstone [...] suggests that "communication is a carp", and that our understanding of it should be premised on the integration of environment and action'[46]. With Silverstone's assistance, Morley touched upon all the mysteries of the trinity of the audience, its action, and its context in the communication process: *communication is a carp*; it is, that is to say, not just an action, but also a context for the action, i.e., the 'real space and time', and 'the daily activities and practices of the individuals and groups',[47] as instructed by the Chinese painters of carp. As for a particular link, that is, the consumption of media mess-

---

45 | Quoted in David Morley, *Television, Audiences and Cultural Studies*, p. 183. Emphasis added.
46 | David Morley, *Television, Audiences and Cultural Studies*, p. 183.
47 | Ibid.

ages, during the process of communication, Silverstone's proposition of 'communication is a carp' is actually proposing to Morley that: to understand what the reception of media messages is, one should not take it as a purely spiritual, intellectual, or epistemological, activity, but as an activity closely associated with or rather, embedded in, the everyday practices of audiences.

The object for audience studies is the *imbedded audience*—given this, the problem will arise that: where is the audience originally before it is 'embedded'? If the audience exists in everyday life from its very beginning and never leaves, how could the *imbedded* audience be imagined and talked about? The 'audience' must have been in the other place, and then it can be embedded. This 'other place' does exist, and it is the epistemology in modern Western philosophy. And the audience that is in the 'other place' also exists and it is, as indicated previously, a purely cognitive subject. It can be said that it is the epistemology that has invented the audience in the 'other place' while the audience is always staying in 'this' place, its own place, having not moved even an inch. The place where the audience lives is its everyday life, a '"natural world", where communication is vague and meanings implicit'[48], but the researchers governed by epistemology attempted to transform the vagueness and implicitness into the 'clarity and objectivity of interpretation' which are embraced by positivism, and opposed to which Morley insisted that 'vagueness is essential to daily patterns of social interaction',[49] and therefore he was determined to re-embed the audience into the '"natural" domestic setting'[50], reviving its nature as the Chinese carp had it. Just as a fish cannot leave water, the audience cannot leave its daily life. If one lifts the audience out of its daily life, this just means to kill it. The audience in epistemology will never be a real audience but a specimen

---

48 | Ibid., p. 185
49 | See David Morley, *Television, Audiences and Cultural Studies*, pp. 184-185.
50 | David Morley, *Television, Audiences and Cultural Studies*, p. 185.

of the audience that has no life. Water means life to a fish, and the vague daily life is the audience's original, natural, and basic life-state.

Perhaps we may have got accustomed to the concept of a purely epistemological 'audience', so when Morley really restored the ordinary life to the audience, taking the audience as its everyday life, we feel it hard to get ourselves accustomed to this. In the normal imagination, the audience is the viewer, who concentrates on television programmes, and who has established the subject-object relationship with television messages. The audience certainly has its daily life, but if the audience does not enter the communication with television programmes, it cannot be categorised as the 'audience'. The audience, as far as it is taken as a concept, must be the subject of knowing, facing the object to be known, which is the media message; or, in the other way round, the audience may be regarded as the object, the receiver and consumer of media messages, and the broadcaster as the subject, the producer and transmitter of media messages. Either as the subject or the object, the audience is situated in a framework of epistemology. This is the same as the theory of *intersubjectivity*, in which although the previous opposition of subject/object has been turned into a reciprocal relation of subject/subject, the truth is: no object, no subject; therefore the framework of epistemology remains unchanged at all. Morley was not willing to put his concept of the audience into this framework; Quite the contrary, as it seemed, Morley was resolute in liberating the audience out of the shackles of this framework.

Could Morley succeed in this or in this way? To step back, does he really intend to do this or this way? To these questions, we cannot simply answer 'yes' or 'no', but what we saw first was his active effort to break through the confinement of epistemology in his audience studies. According to his report, a number of third-hand materials included, television viewing is not an independent or pure activity; it is always interblended with other daily life practices. For example, housewives often watch TV over doing some chores, or chat with friends while watching TV. In such a case, there is no demarcation line between viewing and no-viewing. This is what Morley saw, and the same is in China, and perhaps, everywhere in the world. We have plenty of examples to illustrate this point: there are public televisions at the stations of train or coach, airports, docks, and now increasingly inside the taxis, but viewing in these places is just subsidiary to the travel or associated with other practical activities. Being alone, one may turn on TV, not *watching* it but *listening* to it, to whatever sound it may give out, thereby creating a sense of people being around and getting rid of his or her loneliness. Some people may use TV just for the purpose of easily entering their dreams, and its content is far beyond their concern. And when there is no subject for chatting, TV not only serves as a background, but also provides topics from time to time to enliven the chatting atmosphere. Morley knew clearly that television viewing can mean 'a hundred different things'[51] in everyday life. How many ways the life has, there would be how many ways in which television enters it, but among which, there is no such thing as a *televisional way*! With the eye of Ang, Morley noticed: 'in everyday contexts the distinction between viewing and no-viewing is radically blurred. In day to day reality audience membership is a fundamentally vague subject position; people constantly move in and out of "the TV audience" as they integrate viewing behaviour with a multitude of other concerns and activities in radically contingent ways'[52]. In fact, Ang and then Morley had already realised that: there is no pure television viewing; therefore, there is no audience purely as the subject of viewing. In the history of modern Western philosophy, as widely accepted, the subject was definitely a pure subject, a faculty of knowing, or just to know. But, if it is true, one may be necessarily wondering: how a non-viewing could be *in a way* the epistemological viewing, and in what a way. This needs to be clarified: both Ang and Morley were not able and furthermore did not intend to nullify the audience of television viewing, or, the audience as subject, but

---

51 | Quoted in David Morley, *Television, Audiences and Cultural Studies*, p. 176.
52 | Quoted in David Morley, *Television, Audiences and Cultural Studies*, p. 197.

included the audience of non-viewing, the audience in its everyday life, which, precisely, has yet to be the audience, into the audience of television viewing, and thus the audience of viewing contains the audience of non-viewing. In philosophical terminology, the subject always contains an object inside itself; it is the subject while beyond the subject; it is both subjective and objective. To be clear, the subject can be defined in two ways: first, the subject is imagined as a knowing subject in the domain of epistemology; second, the subject is embodied as a particular individual, a man or a woman, in the domain of real life, which can be termed as the ontological *subject*, or more accurately, which is the origin and substratum for the epistemological subject. Owing to its insistence on the boundary between epistemology and ontology, modern Western philosophy has rarely realised that the distinction between subject and object is only a logical assumption of epistemology. But viewed from the perspective of ontology, the two are actually one; and this 'one' can both *be* and *think*. Morley proposed to include the non-viewing into the viewing, which might appear absurd and preposterous, yet it is with this unusual doing that Morley could impressively reminded us that we should not simply follow modern Western philosophy and ignore the original oneness of subject and object. As Morley's renewed concept of the audience suggested, the subjective audience should introduce its own life, its lived experience, its daily practice, and its domestic context of viewing, into its viewing, which, by contrast, has been for a long time purified as just a mental activity by the philosophy of modernity; thus, the 'audience' is both subjective and objective, both epistemological and ontological; however, in order to know, the subject will *idea*lise, *symbol*ise and *concept*ualise the object, the natural existence of human life, and the naturalised discourses, ideologies, or in one word, the cultural unconscious; speaking reversely, the objective or ontological audience has to undergo a process of *subjectivisation*. In such a case, the viewing and the non-viewing become two poles opposite to each other: one is the knowing that is not equal to the knower; the other is definitely not the object to be known but the determinant of this knowing in a sense that it is the source of the knowing, and furthermore, if the ontological existence of the knower has been epistemologically transformed into the subject, then it is also a determinant in the sense of being part of the knowing if not the largest part. That how far can a knowing go will mainly depend on how far its sources and constituents allow. To know does not mean an interaction between subject and object at a discursive level only, but a dialogue, a negotiation, and a communication between this knowing and that knowing respectively with their sources and internal structures from where they come, which may be called an *ontological dialogue* if it does make sense.

The mystery of why an ontological 'audience' can epistemologically act on media messages has been finally revealed: This is because the audience's ontological existence is *subjectivised* into the audience's epistemological existence, and it also determines the viewing audience as it is the origin and then constituent of this viewing audience. Furthermore, through the long and zigzagged journey of argumentation, we have clearly seen why for Morley the audience can be active: the activeness of the audience does not come from the television viewing, the audience as subject, but from the non-viewing, the audience as its ontological existence, its everyday life, which generates and joins the viewing and thereby determines the viewing. It is just due to the involvement of the non-viewing activities in the viewing that media messages cannot colonise the mind of the audience directly and fully. The media messages and their encoding frameworks have to be interrogated and re-organised by the daily life of the audience before they can do anything substantial to the receivers who are, nevertheless, *de-*coders as Hall implied when he employed the term 'decoding'. One may easily acknowledge a discursive communication, i.e., a communication at a discursive level, between encoders and decoders, but it is hard for him or her to recognise that at the deeper level are the interactions of the realities or material interests, which are brought to light by codes. As suggested earlier, codes cannot change codes in any way, unless through the material existence of the code-makers.

But we should keep it in mind that Morley's conception of the daily practice or the domestic context not only indicates the audience's material existence, but also its discursive existence. Following Morley, Hall and Pêcheux, we have already talked about the 'interdiscursive' existence of the audience or encoders, to which more examples are added now. By quoting K. B. Jensen, Morley reminded us, 'meaning is the stuff that the world of everyday life is made of, individual instances of communication make no sense before they have been interpreted in the total context of the audience's lifeworld'[53]. Mainly associated with Husserl, the concept of 'lifeworld' (*Lebenswelt*) does not point to a natural world, an objective world, or a world in itself, but a man's world, a subjective world, which could be immediately experienced, or a cultural world. Joseph J. Kockelmans paraphrased Husserl's account of 'lifeworld' as follows, against the latter's *The Crisis of European Sciences and Transcendental Phenomenology* which is a most frequently quoted text when Husserl's 'lifeworld' is discussed:

The world indeed includes nature. However, nature is to be understood here as it is given in immediate experience, and not the idealized nature of the physical sciences. But the world comprises more than *mere* nature; there is also 'culture.' Among the beings in the midst of which we find ourselves, there are not only natural beings—objects which may be described exhaustively by pointing to their color, shape, size, or weight—but also tools, instruments, books, buildings, art objects—that is, objects that have human meaning, serve human aims and needs, and satisfy human desires. Because the world has such objects at all and therefore provides the framework within which we live our human life, we refer to it as our life-world (*Crisis*, 127-129 [130-32]).[54]

---

53 | Quoted in David Morley, *Television, Audiences and Cultural Studies*, p. 185.

54 | Joseph J. Kockelmans, *Edmund Husserl's Phenomenology*, West Lafayette, Indiana: Purdue University Press, 1994, p. 337. The '*Crisis*' in the round brackets is the abbreviation of the English edition of Husserl's *The Crisis of European Sciences and Transcendental Phenomenology: An In-*

With reference to Jensen, Morley was trying to argue that a private and domestic world, i.e., a *natural world*, where audiences are embedded, should be a world of meanings. And since meaning always arises from distinction and contestation, namely, from discourse and ideology, Jensen's proposition that 'meaning is the stuff that the world of everyday life is made of' may be altered as '*discourse* is the stuff that the world of everyday life is made of'. Although discourse is not the only stuff of lifeworld or everyday practice, it indeed exists among the stuff and furthermore, it is a *way* of everyday life, a way that organises and directs everyday life at a conscious level. Another example is that, as I understand it, Morley straightforwardly named certain constituents of everyday life: 'it requires to be understood as the dialogical product of inside and outside: of biographies, personalities, meanings, actions, spaces, times, opportunities, and material constrains.'[55] One may simply distinguish these constituents into two kinds: the discursive and the material; or further distinguish one constituent, for instance, 'personalities', into two sub-constituents, but still: the discursive and the material. The third example, which can be regarded as a support to the previous two, is Morley's reference to Hall but of course for his own implication: Hall demanded that cultural studies should include both texts and perhaps what is more important, the tension between texts and other things which are, for instance, 'institutions, offices, agencies, classes, academies, corporations, groups, ideological defined parties, and professions, nations, races and genders'[56]. If ac-

---

troduction to Phenomenological Philosophy, trans. David Carr, Evanston, Ill.: Northwestern University Press, 1970; and the page numbers in the square brackets are that of its German edition: *Die Krisis der europäischen Wissenschaften und die transzendentale Phänomenologie: Eine einleitung in die phänomenologische Philosophie*, ed. Walter Biemel, The Hague: Nijhoff, 1954. Kockelmans' paraphrase of 'lifeworld' is clearer and more accessible than the original account by Husserl himself in *Crisis*.
55 | David Morley, *Television, Audiences and Cultural Studies*, p. 184.
56 | Quoted in David Morley, *Television, Audiences and Cultural Studies*, p. 6.

cording to Althusser, most of these items enumerated by Hall would be counted as ideological apparatuses and their products which, as Morley requested, should be the central concern for 'sociology of television'[57], as the society, into which the television viewing is embedded, is not only *materially* but also *apparatus-ideologically* constituted. As for how to define 'society', a contribution of Althusser's ideological theory is such an assertion, which is yet to be made felt: the 'social existence' is basically material, but it also appears as 'social consciousness'; some kinds of 'social consciousness' that are purely *ideal* may stand sharply opposite to the material 'social existence', while some may be materialised into the materially-featured 'social existence', and these can be termed as *apparatus-ideologies*: they are half material and half ideal. In *society*, discourse, idea, subject, spirit, etc., are all incarnated as realities, entities, apparatuses, or in one word, material forces, and this is the point of William's concept of 'cultural materialism'. In his definition of 'culture', Williams apparently incorporated an elitist conceptualisation of 'culture' by Arnold and Leavis who contended that culture should be intellectual, spiritual, or epistemological if in a philosophical terminology; however, for Williams, once embodied into/as the *material* everyday life, the epistemological culture has already become ontological. This is also the point of the *fundamental* or *philosophical* hermeneutics of Heidegger and Gadamer, which aims to ontologise the concept of *Verstehen* that has been deemed epistemological for long in modern Western philosophy: the *Verstehen* is placed into the 'Überlieferung' which is, in Heidegger's terminology, 'Vorhabe', 'Vorsicht' and 'Vorgriff', or to be brief, 'Vorstruktur', which constitutes our *Dasein*, our *In-der-Welt-sein*, and our daily life. The *Vorstruktur* belongs to a process of *Verstehen*, but this *Verstehen* belongs then to the knowing of the *existents*, the individuals, who exist interrelatedly with others, as Heidegger said: '*Erkennen ist eine Seinsart des In-der-Welt-seins.*'[58] For Heidegger, it is implied that *Erkennen* is a way of life,

57 | See David Morley, *Television, Audiences and Cultural Studies*, p. 6.
58 | Martin Heidegger, *Sein und Zeit*, 18. Aufl., Tübingen: Niemeyer, 2001, S. 61.

a way by which and in which to live, and therefore a way of *In-der-Welt-sein*, and the *In-der-Welt-sein* cannot be *blind* but must be *enlightened* by the *Verstehen* or the *Erkennen*, but which is *fundamentally* part of the *In-der-Welt-sein* in the last analysis. In spite of their different approaches, anthropology for Williams, whilst the 'fundamental ontology' for Heidegger and Gadamer, they were all marching towards transforming the transcendental and elitist conception of 'culture' into the one of everyday life that Morley finally achieved a socio-ontological concept of the audience. This kind of audience is both subject and object, both discourse and the reality that the discourse represents, both social consciousness and social existence, both epistemological *viewing* as a pure knowing and ontological *non-viewing* in everyday life. Thus, once media messages that are encoded so deliberately as to be accepted falls into this mixed and therefore 'vague' audience, there will be numerous decodings to them, among which Hall just indicated three—dominant, negotiated and oppositional. With the audience in everyday life, any decoding can be possible, just as a saying goes: 'There are a thousand Hamlets in a thousand people's eyes.' No exaggeration to say, as soon as codes are broadcasted, they no longer belong to their encoders and senders. The meaning production from codes is the business of the audience, if not exclusively.

But to Morley, just as to Williams, Heidegger, and Gadamer, even if decoding, knowing, or, *Verstehen*, are firmly embedded in society, everyday life, *Dasein*, and *In-der-Welt-sein*, there remains an epistemological issue with them if analytically. Heidegger, for example, committed himself to sweep away the modern epistemology with his fundamental ontology, but which turned out nothing but to move this epistemology from the outside of the *Welt* to the inside of it. Similarly, when Morley put the audience into its domestic or social context, what he did was no more than putting off the explosion of the audience's epistemology. To Morley's *ontological* re-conceptualisation of the *epistemological* audience, we thus still have to question: which one will on earth determine the audience's decoding ultimately: the discourse, or, the unsayable lived being of the bearer of this discourse? Morley only showed the 'context of everyday life' and the 'domestic context' as the determinants of decoding, which, as an answer, remains too rough and general, and needs to be refined and detailed. However, since he, as we have discussed, did not believe that a discourse could run alone and it has to be placed into everyday life, it can be presumed that when he took the audience as its daily practice, he would have already prioritised the audience's daily existence over its discursive existence. Certainly this is the inference from our side. Morley did not explicitly argue this way. This is mainly because it will be hard to isolate discourse, ideology, intellect, spirit, or broadly speaking, culture, from man's material existence: man is by nature a *discursive* animal. In addition, for a sociological research into the audience and its decodings, it would not be necessary and practical as well to analyse a purely material or biological dimension of the audience. However, it should not be forgotten that an anatomy, an abstraction, a clarification, as we did throughout the text, of the 'vague' life of the audience, is traditionally a mission for philosophical studies of any subject.

It needs to be theoretically pointed out that no discourse is able to maintain its impact upon the everyday life of people for good and all. A discourse may be internalised as a way of everyday life, as the cultural unconscious, or, as the political unconscious, but when embedded in the complexity and fluidity of everyday life, it will be definitely changed, or abandoned, or disappear in any way. There is only unchangeable man, but there is no unchangeable culture; and there is only unchangeable instinct, but there is no unchangeable discourse. 'Cultural industry' as a discourse of capitalism may cheat the masses, as the Frankfort school worried about, but which will be only temporary. In the long run, as a popular proverb, originally said by Mao Zedong, goes: 'The masses have sharp eyes!' This is because the masses have Schopenhauer's *will*, or, Freud's *unconscious*, or, Lacan's *réel*, or in one word, their own life, which is the *inner light* if it could be termed as such, which will lead them to go through any discursive darkness, and which, what is most important, can never be deprived by any discourse.

Coda: Chinese Examples

I would like to refer to some Chinese examples to once again illustrate that a discursive force is always limited or fleeting. The first one comes from *The Scholars*, a novel written by Wu Jingzi of the Qing Dynasty.

Once there was a scholar called Wang Yuhui, who was well educated with Confucianism, but which proved not as good as expected. One day, his daughter lost her husband and decided to die for chastity. Yuhui did not oppose her at all but encouraged her to do so: 'Oh, my daughter, you are determined to do so. Why not? This will bring you the fame in the history. I won't stop you! Just do it as you like, please! I will go back home to call your Mum here to bid you adieu.' The daughter fasted to death then. Having got the news, Scholar Wang laughed while saying, with his face towards the sky: 'It's good to die! Good to die!' The daughter was praised as a loyal wife by the government after death and her name was engraved in the Temple for the Virtuous and Chaste Women. However, when Yuhui went sightseeing, he saw a young lady all in white standing on a boat, and he couldn't help but thought of his died daughter. He sobbed at his heart, and tears ran down. Scholar Wang's mind was filled with and dominated by the Confucian discourse of 'chastity', but this discourse could not always maintain its power over him and could not always make him feel honoured. When the natural feeling of family hit him—the honour that had been constructed by the discourse or the discursive honour fell apart at once.

As a story, this was certainly fictionalised by the novelist, but in Chinese history, especially in the time when the Song-Ming Neo-

Confucianism got its ideological hegemony, there were countless stories of such kind that really happened. The Song-Ming Neo-Confucianism educated people with that: 'To die of hunger matters nothing while to lose one's moral integrity matters everything.' Not coincidentally, Scholar Wang's daughter secured her chastity by dying of hunger. She was a lady of moral integrity in the eye of Confucianism! Apparently this story contained Wu Jingzi's sense of irony. This irony revealed that the discourse of 'chastity' promoted by the Song-Ming Neo-Confucianism was challenged in the times of Wu Jingzi. Here we will not refer to those old cases further, but turn to a case close to our times.

During the 10 years' calamity of the so-called 'Great Cultural Revolution' (1966-1976), many people went mad, ill-treating and killing each other, because their brains had been washed by the false propaganda discourse of that time. But when the havoc was over, many of them repented immediately for their wrong doings in the past. The confession if not so religious was a fascinating topic shortly after the 'Revolution', which is still attracting the attention of intellectuals now. As fascism in Germany was just an episode in history, the discourse of the 'Great Cultural Revolution' is no longer dominating in China. There is indeed a limit to the discourse, but we did not discern it when the discourse was in its heyday. This is simply due to that we were staying inside the discourse, as represented by two Chinese poetic lines:

The true face of Mount Lushan cannot be known,
When you are in rather than beyond the mountain.

There is a true Mount Lushan which is far beyond us, and there is as well a discursive Mount Lushan in which we are staying. We are always deceived, oppressed and poisoned by the discourse of Mount Lushan or the discursive Mount Lushan, but we are always happy with it when within it. To know the truth, to resist or overthrow the discourse, if we have failed in all other ways, the last resort, which never fails, is our own life, to be exact, the life in itself, rather than the life in a way, in an *order*, therefore an ordinary life, or in the terminology of psychoanalysis, the instinct, which has not yet been *ordered* and *encoded*, and which has escaped or transcended the discursive Mount Lushan.

We are very grateful to David Morley, and Stuart Hall, who may not agree to our conclusion, but have helped us to arrive at it, at least in the vein of this text.

Appendix 1. Towards Global Dialogism
Transcending 'Cultural Imperialism' and Its Critics

Abstract Cultural studies has developed from its domestic stage into the present international stage, and a new theoretical framework is accordingly demanded. In other words, international cultural studies should have its own theoretical platform corresponding to its internationality. Based mainly upon the dispute around 'cultural imperialism', this essay categorises cultural studies into two modes, the 'modernity' cultural studies and the 'post-modernity' cultural studies, analysing their advantages and disadvantages respectively, and suggests as the third mode the 'globality' cultural studies that transcends the previous two, the tenet of which is a philosophy of *global dialogism* that sublates (*aufheben*) both modernity and postmodernity at one time.

Key Words cultural studies, modernity, postmodernity, globalization, global dialogism

1. Globalization as a New Philosophy

It is increasingly realised that globalization is not only an object we face, but also, more importantly, a perspective we should employ to look at all the phenomena stemming therein. This is to say, among the consequences of globalization, a philosophical one is looming and figuring: globalization is to be a new philosophical concept transcending modernity and postmondernity and their binary opposition. It is modernity, and postmodernity as well, and to be precise, it is them two simultaneously, and a complicatedly dynamic relationship between them.

This epochal proposition, which should have been developed by philosophers, is now, nevertheless, alluded to us by sociologists. In the concluding chapter of *The Consequences of Modernity*, Anthony Giddens thus summarises: 'One of the fundamental consequences of modernity[...]is globalisation. This is more than a diffusion of Western institutions across the world, in which other cultures are crushed. Globalisation—which is a process of uneven development that fragments as it coordinates—introduces new forms of world interdependence, in which, once again, there are no "others" [...] Is modernity peculiarly Western from the standpoint of its globalising tendencies? No. It cannot be, since we are speaking here of emergent forms of world interdependence and planetary consciousness.' (1990: 175) Giddens does not deny the modernity aspect of globalization, that is, the imperial project spread to the whole world by Western institutions; he tends more, however, to see the failure of this grand project in its process of implementation and the interdependence between nations/states resulted from this failure—different from Giddens, we call this the 'postmodernity' dimension of globalization, and this is in a way what he states elsewhere: globalization will result in a 'runaway world' (2002: xxxi).

As regards globalization as 'postmodernity', John Tomlinson's radically playful stance is likely to appall any theorist if he or she is seriously minded. In his stir-making monograph *Cultural Imperialism* (first published in 1991), Tomlinson seems to have an abundance of confidence to exterminate, once for all, the view of globalization as 'modernity':

Globalisation may be distinguished from imperialism in that it is a far less coherent or culturally directed process. For all that it is ambiguous between economic and political senses, the idea of imperialism contains, at least, the notion of a purposeful project: the *intended* spread of a social system from one centre of power across the globe. The idea of 'globalisation' suggests interconnection and interdependency of all global areas which happens in a far less purposeful way. It happens as the result of economic and cultural practices which do not, of themselves, aim at global integration, but which nonetheless produce it. More importantly, the effects of globalisation are to weaken the cultural coherence of all individual nation-states, including the economically powerful ones—'the imperialist powers' of a previous era. (2001: 175)

Tomlinson, however, cannot prove to us, even minimally, that globalization, regardless of its consequences, is simply a spontaneous process without any motivator. This would not be the case, unless globalization has nothing to do with human beings as agents. Obviously, Tomlinson's mistake is to disregard the *intentions* to globalize with the *consequences* of globalization. He seems to be ignorant of the fact that 'intention' is subjective while 'consequence' is objective. Since globalization is driven by human beings with *intentions*, the 'modernity' aspect of it cannot be denied. Giddens' term 'runaway world', if compared with Tomlinson's radicalism, would be far better to describe globalization, because it not only verifies that some one is trying to control (*intentionally*) but at the same time sees that he or she fails to control the world (*consequently*).

Borrowing a Japanese term, *dochakuka*, Roland Robertson calls globalization *glocalization*, a condensed form of global localization (1992: 173-174), by which he means that globalization is a process of interaction between the global and the local. 'Its central *dynamic* involves the twofold process of the particularization of the universal and the universalization of the particular.' (1992: 177-178) Robertson's approach to globalization, as we know it, is mainly from the perspectives of religion, ideology or in general, culture, and as such is more philosophically pertinent. In the context of globalization, we cannot speak only of the local, nor can we replace the local with the global, the dialectic of which indicates a philosophical question of universality and particularity appearing in any specific instance.

To be brief, globalization in the vision of the current sociological studies has already outlined for us a complete philosophical map of the complicated relationship between modernity and postmodernity: modernity is the philosophy of subjectivity since Descartes, while postmodernity the concept of 'intersubjectivity' raised by Husserl after his realisation of the drawback of egoism in his philosophy of subjectivity, and also 'communicative rationality' later developed by Habermas. Whether adopting the term 'postmodernity' or not, any theory critical towards the philosophy of a modern subject can be viewed, in a way, as an awareness of 'postmodernity' that attempts to transcend modernity. Postmodernity used to be mistaken as a form of nihilism by Giddens, and Habermas, among many others; but in its reality, it is nothing but a radical Husserianism. Derrida, for example, reminds us how all those items we term as consciousness, language and culture, are structures in the framework of reason that has obscured the truth we are seeking and hence they are to be 'suspended' for 'phenomenological reduction'. Postmodernity, therefore, is a renewed form of epistemology and a redirected way of reflectivity that sweep up the fog of modernity. If 'postmodernity' appears to be a total abandonment of reason and its corresponding truth because of its harsh critique of the latter, globalization as a new philosophy, then, would maintain subjectivity, rationality, universality and the ultimate of modernity, but at the same time explore their limitations by taking into consideration such issues as Other, body, particularity, singularity and process. Or, to put it differently, globalization doesn't simply identify itself with modernity, nor does it with postmodernity; rather, it stands on the endless opposition or antagonism between them, on an *articulation* that is forever unsettled. Lack of either dimension, it won't be called 'globalization', and we won't be able to correctly understand globalization, a new object to us, and all the phenomena that have happened in the era of globalization.

2. The 'Globality' Cultural Studies in the Era of Globalization

The British history of cultural studies, if dated back to 1958, when Williams published his *Culture and Society*, has passed half a century. Cultural studies in the beginning was a British domestic enterprise, devoted to targeting its domestic cultural and political problems, such as mass media, popular culture, youth sub-culture, and consumer society, etc., within which Marxism, ideology, hegemony, resistance and articulation were its key words, or, one might say, the soul of cultural studies. Approximately since the 1990's, the topics of cultural studies have been rapidly internationalised. Stuart Hall began to talk about identity, hybridity, new ethnicity, Britishness, and globalization, though he also mentioned them from time to time in his earlier years. An inspection of the conceptual history of David Morley's media studies will show that in the 1980's the terms he was most interested in are 'nationwide' (audience), 'family' (television), and 'domestic' (viewing context), while since the 1990's, then, he has changed his topics into such ones like 'global media, electronic landscapes, and cultural boundaries', 'home territories' and 'cosmopolitics' that are particular to or brought to the foreground by globalization. More strikingly, in recent years, such buzzwords like 'global culture', 'global citizen', and 'global public space' have painted the *globality* of cultural studies with a blaze of colours, and signified for it a rampant spring.

The publication of *The International Journal of Cultural Studies* (since 1998), and the global flourishing of the university courses and departments in the name of 'cultural studies' across the world, some of which are, especially, under the advertising banner of 'international cultural studies', have all included cultural studies into the context of globalization *institutionally*.

A sharp voice, as raised by a group of authors in their collaborative book, for *Globalizing Cultural Studies* (McCarthy *et al.*, 2007), with a strong motive to put an end to 'that traditional British, sub-cultural models of cultural studies', 'both methodological and interpretive', which, they are jubilant to see, 'have been exhausted, rendered archaic by the monumental, shifting of global conditions and multiple diasporic figurations that exist in the contemporary moment' (Denzin, 2007: XII), is now moving steadily to the fore.

All signs, to mention above just a few, indicate that cultural studies has *consciously* entered a global stage. However, this does not necessarily mean that cultural studies has already acquired a clear and proper 'consciousness of globality'. No one will negate that the future cultural studies will definitely be global, which, however, is at the same time a requirement at a deeper level, that is, cultural studies in the global age, advancing with the time, must have 'globalization' or 'globality' as a philosophical concept to be its new theory, new mind and new horizon, or it would remain a 'modernity' cultural studies or a 'postmodernity' cultural studies, rather than the 'global cultural studies' or the 'globality' cultural studies that will synthesise and then transcend both modernity and postmodernity philosophically.

Taking the debate over 'cultural imperialism' as an example, we are to expound hereafter what is the 'modernity' cultural studies and the 'postmodernity' cultural studies respectively, and to investigate where their particular problems lie in. Lastly, with the philosophically-renewed concept of 'globality', which we would foreground as *global dialogism*, we will re-observe the phenomenon of cultural flows referred by the dispute of 'cultural imperialism', which doesn't just start from today, nay, we may even say, from the remote time of Plato or Confucius. Culture has never stopped its flowing. Culture is always clashing, dividing, merging, and looking for new heterogeneities to merge with. No national culture today is born independent, and even nation itself is not of one single origin. Globalization, however, has brought this ever-told story before us with new urgency and problematicness, to which, we cannot face with ease.

3. The 'Postmodernity' Cultural Studies Doesn't Acknowledge 'Cultural Imperialism'

Let us now first examine the 'postmodernity' cultural studies, its representations and problems.

Tomlinson's *Cultural Imperialism* would be considered a model instance if we can categorise it into the 'postmodernity' cultural studies. It is systemic, deep and logical and has inflicted great casualties to its adversaries. Since then, it seems, 'cultural imperialism' has collapsed and never returned to the fore of cultural theory.

The 'cultural imperialism' thesis, to put it simply, refers to such an argument that a culture, Western culture of course, or American culture, has completely conquered and reorganised another culture, the weaker culture, to be sure, especially the Third World culture, into a certain unitary 'imperial' culture. To fight against this, Tomlinson has resorted to many kinds of weapons, among which, the most powerful one is the interactive theory between text and reader that comes from philosophical hermeneutics or reception-aesthetics.

Tomlinson does not hide himself from the phenomenon of how American culture represented by Disney cartoons, Hollywood movies, McDonald fast food and the Levi jeans has conquered in other cultures via export, which is a fact no one can deny; yet Tomlinson turns away from that and raises this question: 'But the key question is, does this presence represent cultural imperialism?' For him, 'Clearly the sheer presence *alone* does not', because 'A text does not become culturally significant until it is read. Until it is read it has the same status as imported blank paper: a material and economic significance, but not a directly cultural significance. At this level of analysis, then, reading the imperialism text becomes the crucial issue in judging cultural imperialism.' (2001: 42) From the reception theory as understood by Tomlinson, the so called 'cultural imperialist' texts signify nothing at all before they are read; even if they signify, their significance is not the original one after they have been read. The cultural significance of a text is, therefore, a later creation by the reader.

Tomlinson chooses the effect study of the TV serial *Dallas* carried out by Tamar Liebes and Elihu Katz to support his denial of 'cultural imperialism'. According to Liebes and Katz, 'The name of *Dallas* in the 1980s became a metaphor for the conquest of the world by an American television serial. *Dallas* signifies an international congregation of viewers (one of the largest in history), gathered once weekly to follow the saga of the Ewing dynasty—its interpersonal relations and business affairs.' (1993: 5) Such effect of *Dallas* is usually viewed as a unique event of cultural imperialism, a delivering and reception of the 'cultural meaning' of American imperialism. In view of the theorists of 'cultural imperialism', such is its trajectory: 'hegemony is prepackaged in Los Angeles, shipped out to the global village, and unwrapped in innocent minds.'(1993: xi) Liebes and Katz aim to examine the argument of 'cultural imperialism' with their investigations of audiences' actual responses. To Tomlinson's great delight, their empirical studies show that: 'Audiences are more active and critical, their responses more complex and reflective, and their cultural values more resistant to manipulation and "invasion" than many critical media theorists have assumed.' (2001: 49-50) Indeed, the effect research of Liebes and Katz proves that 'Decoding is an interaction between the culture of the viewers and the culture of the producer' (1993: x), this therefore subverts the hypothesis, as quoted above, of 'cultural imperialism' regarding the meaning of the texts made by the theorists of 'cultural imperialism', that is, viewing it as a linear process of transportation.

Yet Tomlinson has forgotten, or he may not realise, that the philosophical hermeneutics or the reception-aesthetics belongs to Husserl's phenomenology; they are postmodern, but not simply 'postmodern'. Meaning is the consequence of the *interaction* between the text and the reader, not just coming from the reader. Those who have ever read of Gadamer, Hans Robert Jauss or Wolfgang Iser would not make such a misunderstanding of no sense. Even within the 'postmodern' theories, Derrida's deconstruction, for example, there is no such assertion that 'anything goes' with the meaning of text; only the 'Tomlinsonian Postmodern' is an exception.

We will let it pass if this is but one example, what is worse, however, is that such argument that denies 'cultural imperialism' through a hermeneutic reading has almost become a dominant view in the field of media research by way of Tomlinson's seemingly persuasive and forceful argumentation. There appears thus a vision that the discourse of 'cultural imperialism' is beheaded and its bleeding head is hung high on the city wall, against the chilly wind, openly declaring the inviolable justice and rule of the 'postmodernity' cultural studies.

We are greatly astonished to see that in recent years, in Germany, where there is a long tradition of phenomenology, there are such scholars that follow the extremeness and shallowness of Tomlinson to strengthen and push forward the postmodern understanding of global culture. Ulrich Beck, Professor of Sociology at the University of Munich, in one of his newly published article (2003: 16-29)[1], states that 'the concept of *Americanization* is based on a national understanding of globalization' which he criticises as a form of 'methodological nationalism'. As an alternative program, he suggests that globalization must be understood as 'cosmopolitanization' that is 'capable of reflecting a newly transnational world'. According to his etymological study, *cosmopolitan*, the core of *cosmopolitanizaion*, is made up of two roots: 'cosmos' and 'polis', the former meaning 'nature' and the latter 'city/state'. The combined word 'cosmopolitan' shows that every human being is rooted by birth in two worlds, one is nature, and the other is the limited, like city, boundary, ethnicity and religion. The principle of globalization as 'cosmopolitanization' is not 'either/or', but 'this-as-well-as-that'. 'cosmopolitanism generates a logic of non-exclusive oppositions', according to which, 'nature is associated with society, the object is a part of subjectivity, otherness of the other is included in one's own self-identity and self-definition, and the logic of exclusive oppositions is rejected' and replaced by the 'inclusive oppositions', that is, all oppositions are included in a larger framework, which is 'nature', or 'cosmos', or 'universe', or 'oneness', or 'absolute'.

For fear of being mistaken as re-garmented universalism, Beck adds the term 'rooted' before 'cosmopolitanism', in order to emphasise this 'universe's acceptance of difference, opposition, individuality and locality. Because of his emphasis on 'universe', on 'universe's controlling of the versatile, the plural, and the various, Beck does not allow us to imagine globalization as an inter-relationship between nations which have been taken before as independent units, for example, the concept of 'interconnectedness' by the British sociologist David Held, not to mention the word 'international' that we have long been used to; they must be discarded altogether.

Yet what is difficult for Beck is, firstly, such a 'universe' is but an 'imaginative community', or, even if it does exist, it must be constructed by the imagination of the 'rooted' individuals. It won't do unless it is local, historical, national and ideological, thus that is difficult for it to be pure, objective, enjoying the identification of the whole body of the individuals.

This means, secondly, in its ultimate sense, the individual cannot be forsaken simply because any consciousness, for instance, the consciousness of 'universe', must first be lodged physically; consciousness is the consciousness of the individual, without whom, who is to imagine the 'universe'? Even when in the future, the world may achieve the *Great Sameness*, a utopia created by Laozi, an ancient Chinese sage, the individuality and uniqueness of the individual won't disappear in such a world of sameness.

Via the 'cosmopolitanism' re-interpreted with new loadings, Beck denies 'Americanization' that is based on the unitary thinking of nation, which would also be a refusal to 'cultural imperialism', an invention of, for him, same way of thinking. Thirdly, however, as 'cosmopolitanism' still assumes the existence of the contradiction and opposition between nations and locals, if they are not equal and well-matched in strength, there must be one side which is more advantageous over the other side or other sides, be it Gramsci's soft 'hegemony' or Lenin's violent 'dictatorship', there then abides the existence of 'cultural imperialism'. Not false at all, 'Americanization' or 'cultural imperialism' is based on a premise of a national understanding of globalization. This premise, nevertheless, cannot be erased unless the national contradictions and conflicts arising from global communication are ignored, unless the individual, as well as human being, is eliminated, then can we return the 'universe' that is primal, chaotic and without distinction between the heaven and the earth. In the era of globalization, the abiding efficiency of 'cultural imperialism' lies in its assumption of the irremovability of nation and local in the global communication. Furthermore, it assumes the eternal existence of the individual. The 'transnationality' of 'the second modernization' cannot end the 'nationality' of 'the first modernization', at least at present, and in the foreseeable future. 'Modernity' will pass through 'postmodernity' and enter 'globality'; it will surely reorient itself in its adaptation to the postmodern condition.

It must be noted that although Beck's 'cosmopolitanism' is, allegedly, still to recognise opposition, difference, nationality and individual, yet because he includes them into the category of a 'cosmos', a 'universe', making all these the so-called 'inclusive oppositions', such opposite elements have lost their original meanings and are no longer themselves. With Beck, another expression for 'cosmopolitanism' is 'transnationality'. Same as with that in the 'cosmos', although in the logic of 'transnationality' there still exists nationality, yet because there is no longer the 'one-to-one-correspondence' between these nations, they have to instead talk to the 'universe', which means the afore talk-to-each-other is now elevated to a simultaneous talk to the 'universe', that is to say, they surpass their nationalities and dialogise with the 'universe', accepting its norms and restrictions. They talk to each other, no problem, but all the each-others are to transcend themselves, so that they, all the each-others, would be *universalised*. The '*trans*-nationalization' is then nothing but a *de*-nationalisation, the '*cosmo*-politanisation' a *de*-politanisation, consigning, with the introduction of something *transcendent*, the nation and the polis to oblivion. According to Beck, even 'as soon as the euro was introduced', or even 'To the extent that Europe exists, there is no longer any such thing as Germany, or France, or Italy, or Britain, and so on' (Beck,

2005: xi). 'The premise' for 'cosmopolitanism,' Beck contends, 'here is that the national is ceasing to be the national'. To logically go a bit further, for Beck, since 'nation' or 'state' has disappeared, where can 'Americanization' be, and where can 'cultural imperialism' exist? In the era of globalization, there is no such an agent like 'America' to carry out 'Americanization', and no 'nation' to implement 'cultural imperialism'!

At this point, we may say that Beck is quite 'postmodern', though he may not be in favour of such labeling. With a usual approach in postmodern *philosophy* that he puts the 'subject' of modernity into a 'structure', more precisely, Derrida's 'structure without centre', and erases its 'subjectivity', its suppression and integration of others, *sociologically* then he abolishes 'Americanization' and 'cultural imperialism'. A 'structure', as we know it, is always of *transcendence*: transcending all the individuals through *structuring* this individual with another, another individual, which is, but, said to be the *structure*, and the former is then no longer an individual, but an integrated part of the structure, or vice versa for the latter. But please don't forget, the transcending one is always *another*, ever-making one journey further away! In a structure, all are against all *as individuals or subjects*. They structure and deconstruct each other. No individual or subject can survive a structure! By the way, it may not be too late to add here, among the various reasons for Tomlinson to abolish 'cultural imperialism', there is also such a postmodern doing, which, though, is not so *structurally* and *transcendently* as Beck does, to remove 'nation', 'nation-state', 'individual' and 'subject' so that there will be 'no way/no one' to 'Americanize' and 'no way/no one' to carry out 'cultural imperialism'.

If it is by the *transcendent refusal* to the philosophical 'subject' and the sociological 'nation' that Beck removes 'Americanization' and 'cultural imperialism', what would be puzzling is that Rainer Winter, a leading cultural theorist in the German-speaking world, removes 'cultural imperialism' through the *immanent affirmation* of 'subject', 'individual', and 'context'—all in all, the affirmation of what I would call 'situational hermeneutics', which is, needless to say, in an opposite direction to Beck's. Since they hold different 'Roads', how can a same destination be reached? It must be remembered that such 'Roads' are not those trivial 'methods'.

In his article (2003: 206-221)[2] that appears in the same collection with Beck's, to refute the view that popular culture dominated by the USA will result in the cultural standardisation and stereotypisation and the disappearance of the uniqueness of the local culture, Winter quotes broadly from many cultural resources, with *Rambo* and *Dallas*, especially with his own investigation of the spread and reception of hip hop music enthusiastically promoted by American culture industry as examples, and proves that such global media products have not led to the situations mentioned above, on the contrary, he agrees with the famous observation of Arjun Appadurai: 'the consumption of the mass media throughout the world often provokes resistance, irony, selectivity, and in general, *agency*.' (1996: 7)[3]. Winter firmly believes that to consume is to enter 'the processes of de-territorialization, syncretization and hybridization', and to accept is to appropriate, to express, to produce and to practice. What interests Winter is that the consumption and reception of the so-called texts of 'cultural imperialism' appears to be an active counter-process, a process of subjecting all the subjections from them if they have.

Such is the 'dialectics of globalization', or as he said in the co-authored 'Introduction' to the collection we mentioned above, the 'cultural consequence of globalization', that is, 'Starting from the phenomenon of Americanization', and followed by the 'cultural consequence of globalization' (Natan Sznaider and Rainer Winter, 2003: 3). With this, Winter and other cultural sociologists have already given comprehensive and persuasive argumentation with huge amounts of field work, I think, however, a further job should be done, i.e., to *theoretically* lay bare—we need to get into the whys and wherefores—that: how can *cultural imperialism*, if there is such a thing at the very beginning, result in such unexpected outcomes? Where may the power that is capable of resisting 'cultural imperialism' come from? Winter in his article does not answer such questions. Through a careful reading, however, we seem to be able to infer that, first, the consumer is a 'subject' or 'individual', or an 'individual subject', who has his/her own interests and intellects; second, the consumer has his/her own 'context' or 'local', and such 'context' and 'local' are not merely the outside environment for his/her actions, but have long been internalised as the consumer's most authentic life being as an 'individual subject'; third, the consumer has his/her own coding system, more importantly, his/her own daily life practice. To sum up, the consumer must be recognised as an 'individual'. From this fundamental sense, Winter draws the conclusion from his ethnographic investigations that through the hip hop series of products, hip hoppers 'define their own personal individual identity and hence, for *individualization*' (italicised mine). What goes without saying for Winter is that only by being an 'individual', can the consumer *individualise* media commodities.

Regarding Beck's removal of 'cultural imperialism' with 'cosmopolitanism', we can say without hesitation that his model is the 'postmodernity' cultural studies, because he has deconstructed the idea of the 'individual subject', which is at the core of modern values. As for Winter and the peers he has quoted from, and Tomlinson *in part* because he sometimes stands in this 'situational hermeneutics', we cannot not generalise them together. Respectively, scholars like Winter adopt different perspectives to the consumers and producers of text messages: to look for the power to transform, to resist or to overthrow the texts of 'cultural imperialism', they recognise the 'modernity' of the consumers, that is, they look at the consumers as the in-self and for-self 'individual' or 'cultural individual'; but with the 'cultural imperialists', who are producers of 'imperialist texts' and should be treated as 'individual subjects' as well, Winter and the critics on his side are silent, rather, they are keen to *postmodernly* put them into 'intersubjectivity' or, 'trans-subjectivity', which perhaps works with Beck who already has the similar term 'transnationality', and thus de-subjectivise them.

For Winter and his supporters, as long as 'cultural imperialism' is treated the way the consumer is treated, it will definitely lead to the recognition of the 'modernity' cultural studies. The problem is, however—

4. Where There Is The 'Modernity' Cultural Studies, There Is 'Cultural Imperialism'

This is an ironic logic. We do not believe that scholars like Winter would have overlooked that 'cultural imperialists' should also be treated as 'individual subjects'. Quite the opposite, they should have known it very well. But the problem just lies in that if they have taken this into consideration, their theory of anti-'cultural imperialism' would face the possibility of collapsing. However, we must not ignore a completeness of the fact for the sake of an imagined completeness of a theory. Doing cultural studies in the era of globalization, we cannot rashly give up its 'modernity' model, instead, there are enough reasons why we cannot totally negate it.

For the 'modernity' cultural studies, what is straightforward is that as long as we recognise the global encoders and the local decoders both as limited 'cultural individuals', recognise their respective existence as 'nations' (born as such, etymologically), there must exist 'Americanization' or 'cultural imperialism'.

Beck tries to disintegrate 'city/state' with 'nature' and to remove 'nationality' with 'transnationality'. However, those on the side of the 'modernity' cultural studies can often successfully point out the vanity of 'nature', 'transnationality', and all the other theories under the banner of 'universalism'. Marxists insist that the social existence determines the social consciousness and the economic foundation the upper structure. In spite of many complicated links among them, be it G. V. Plekhanov's 'social psychology' or Williams' 'culture', none can change the last determination of the former over the latter. Therefore, it can be held that any theory or proposition that is trying to surpass a certain social existence and economic foundation, is at a deeper level but a reflection of the social existence and economic foundation it comes from. It is ideology. Classic Marxists long ago exposed the hypocrisy of the bourgeoisie in its 'liberty', 'equality' and 'fraternity'. Today, in the era of globalization, the 'specters of Marx' (Derrida), whether in the Third World like China and India or the First World like Britain, France, and Germany, are proving that the so-called 'universal culture' propagandised by America or the West is nothing more than American-ness or Western-ness, or in one word, 'locality'. To put it further, they are proving that there exists no 'global value' but 'global interests' and that 'global value' is always deployed as a chessman in the game of 'global strategies'. This is no secret and no one is ignorant of or does not understand the principle of 'the supremacy of the national interests'; 'international' diplomacy is far from 'internationalism', it is nothing but the maximisation of the nation's interests in its negotiation with other countries. Jesus says that where your treasure is, where your heart will be; and we will say that where your treasure is, where your point of speaking will be. All circles around interests and the discourse is no exception.

At this point, we might point out that Nietzsche and the 20th century postmodern theorists who aligned themselves with Marx temporarily, have long ago destroyed the distinctions between 'interpretation' and 'fact', 'discourse' and 'truth', 'narrative' and 'history', 'signifier' and 'signified', 'culture' and 'nature', etc. They find that the disconnection and contradiction between them are innate and therefore cannot be overcome. Foucault, among them, evidences historically that 'discourse' is in essence 'power', the 'will to power', the 'will to life', and does not necessarily correspond with 'truth'. According to the old Schopenhauer, the *Vorstellung* is but that of the *Wille* itself. Schopenhauer's *Vorstellung* is here revived by Foucault's 'discourse'. After all, it is desire that speaks; it speaks via a 'discourse'.

The relationship between British cultural studies and postmodernism has always been ambiguous. In the deconstruction of high culture, the insistence on the difference and hybridity, the critical attitude towards Occidentalism, and the rejection of the concept of 'culture industry', etc., it seems that British cultural studies and postmodernism understand and appreciate each other, however, the difference in their starting points covered by the same aim must also be noted: the theoretical resource for post/structuralism, the core of postmodernism, is Saussure's semiotics, especially its potential to deconstruct subjectivity, in which the signifier only points to another signifier, and the signifying activity is but a floating chain made up of pure signifiers, therefore the so-called speaking 'subject' becomes that being spoken—spoken by the signifiers, by culture, by tradition, etc.; it is the spokesman—speaking for others and cannot speak itself or speak about itself. In modern philosophy, as with Kant, the 'subjectivity' of the subject comes from its determination of the object. The postmodern theorists turn this round and the subject is now determined by the object and stops being the subject. To acknowledge or not the subjectivity forms the most important watershed in philosophy between modernity and postmodernity. While for British cultural studies, though it is not always so (because of its utilitarian attitude toward theory and the resulting lack of notice of the inner coherence of theory), at least in its research on the media audience that is pertinent to 'cultural imperialism', the most important theoretical support is its insistence on the subjectivity, concretely, its treatment of the media audience as the discourse subject, and more importantly, the individual subject. David Morley, who is well known for his active audience theory, early in the 1970s pointed out that 'we must not see the audience as an undifferentiated mass but as a complex structure, made up of a number of overlapping subgroups, each with its own history and cultural traditions.' (1974: 8) He demands an investigation of the audience's 'position in the class structure', their 'regional situation', 'ethnic origin', 'age' and 'sex', which are the primary factors in sociology (1974: 8-9). This also means that he needs a more concrete concept of 'audiences'. Directly influenced by Hall and indirectly by Althusser, the young Morley then does not quite agree to treat the audience further as respective individuals. In his later researches on the '*Nationwide* audience' and 'family TV', however, he actually synthesises the sociological analysis with individual analysis. More importantly, he ontologises the reception context of the audience, that is, the ontological existence of the audience. Hall is strongly against private readings, yet when he says 'different groups and classes of people will bring different explanatory frameworks to bear' (1973b: 12), he has already treated the audience as 'social individual' or 'individual collective'. In Morley's researches on the media audience, in Hall's theory of encoding/decoding, in their treatment of the audience as 'subject', we may assert that British cultural studies belongs to the 'modernity' cultural studies.

If we move the audience theory of the early (1970s) British cultural studies from its domestic context into an observation of the global media, like what Winter suggests, i.e., putting cultural studies into a sociology of hybridity formations (2003), it would be definitely anti-'cultural imperialism'. Such 'appropriation' of or 'resistance' to 'cultural imperialism' is quite different from Beck's and Tomlinson's 'postmodernity' cultural studies that is based on the deconstruction of 'subjectivity'. Hall has never given up the 'structure' of Althusser, for him, all negotiated and oppositional or resistant decoding in mass communication are under the constraint of the 'communicative structure' in one way or another: 'Production and reception of the television message are, not[...]identical, but they are related: they are differentiated moments within the totality formed by the communicative process as a whole.' (1973a: 3) In his later investigation of 'global mass culture', Hall still holds his early idea concerning the 'structure'[4]. He finds that on the one hand, 'it is centered in the West and it always speaks English' and on the other, such English is no longer the 'Queen's English' or 'highbrow English', it becomes 'an international language which is quite a different thing'. English is scattered now. Furthermore, 'It is a homogenizing form of cultural representation, enormously absorptive of things, as it were, but the homogenization is never absolutely complete, and it does not work for completeness.' (1991a: 28) Hall also calls this structure, the 'structure' of Althusser's, as Gramsci's 'hegemony'; true, 'hegemony' exists and tries to enclose all within itself, yet 'hegemony' can never be completed (1991b: 68). Similarly, for Hall, as Winter (2003: 218) has noticed, though Hall on the one hand does not think that the global flows of sign, information and images can produce a standardised culture, and on the other he sees a new homogenisation emerging through the global process of commercialisation. Obviously, not far back from the 'structure', 'hegemony', or 'the new dialectics of global culture' (1991a: 19), another expression of Hall, there shines Hall's firm belief in the philosophy of modernity's 'subjectivity'. Different from Althusser, Hall puts into this borrowed 'structure' difference, contradiction, struggle and therefore the endless opening of the structure—with modernity he 'deconstructs' the postmodern-orientated 'structure/deconstruction'. It is Hall's prediction that among all the new forms of globalization, there abides the antagonism between control and anti-control—'That old dialectic is not at an end. Globalization does not finish it off.' (1991a: 39) The reason for this is the eternal existence of the controller and the anti-controller as 'rooted' individual. Unless the 'individual' and 'subject' are uprooted, the 'modernity' cultural studies will stick to its theory of 'resistance' and 'struggle'.

Hall's 'structure' view of cultural communication sets the direction of British cultural studies, that is, the 'modernity' cultural studies. It also specifically sets agenda for Morley's 'active audiences'. But, let us then lay aside Hall for a moment and talk about Morley. True, Morley's conception 'active audiences', if translated to the global media, will become a theory against 'cultural imperialism'. However, there remain two problems: first, its antagonism towards 'cultural imperialism' is from *effect*, not from *intention* because, like audiences, the motivators of 'cultural imperialism' are local, individual and subjective, for whom, we cannot imagine an action of 'cultural imperialism' without the *intention* of 'cultural imperialism', which not only violates the proposition that human are rational animals and betrays the fact, be it historical or contemporary. In consequence, the theory of 'active audiences' must admit the capitalist *intention* of 'culture industry' at the domestic level, and the cultural strategy of 'capital imperialism' at the international level, a cultural strategy motivated by *interests*. In other words, 'active audiences' can neither replace 'culture industry', nor can it deny 'cultural imperialism'.

Secondly, perhaps what is more theoretically fundamental, 'active audiences' must put 'individual' and 'subject' advocated by it into the framework of 'inter-subjectivity'. As long as the encoders are also viewed as subjects, reception is surely to be an 'inter-subjective' event; as long as a subject enters 'inter-subjectivity', the dialogical process with another subject, it will surely be modified more or less. Moreover, this is beyond one's intention because the presence of another subject or just an other will objectively change the existing environment of the subject and the environment is life-ontological. Semiologically, the 'inter-textuality' provides the 'text' with a 'context' and the autonomy of the text is thus broken, that is, the text is not what it was. The same relationship exists between the encoders' 'global' texts and the decoders' 'local' texts: because of the global encoders, the local decoders will be no longer as local as it was before.

Let us now come back to Hall. More thoughtful and sophisticated than Morley, Hall includes cultural imperialism and the antagonism towards it, as well as the dialectic movement between the global and the local once and for all into the dynamic concept of 'structure' and foresees the future culture, exampled by modern music, is 'the aesthetics of the hybrid, the aesthetics of the crossover, the aesthetics of the diaspora, the aesthetics of creolization' (1991a: 38-39). Hall's cultural studies of the global culture, in its insistence and implement of the principle of subjectivity, belongs to modernity philosophy. We are delighted to see that with the concept of 'structure', Hall has elaborated modernity's insight regarding global culture all down to its extreme, that is, in the framework of modernity, he has predicted the final bankruptcy of the project of cultural imperialism, which has surpassed modernity and has postmodern propensity. Yet this postmodernity is surely different from that of French post/structuralism.

For globalization in a larger space, however, Hall's vision might be a little narrow. In the process of colonisation, which is, among others, one form of modernisation, Hall sees hybrid culture appearing in ex-colonies and ex-suzerain states. How about other countries and regions, especially those on different roads to modernisation? This limited vision, the postcolonial vision, will bring and has already brought certain blindness to the future cultural forms, for instance, can hybridity only be treated as a finished form rather than an ever-hybridising process? It might be so in ex-colonies, and in America, the biggest ex-colony, partly so; yet in suzerain states it might not be so, and in countries like China and Japan, Hall's 'hybrid' may have totally different meanings. What is helpful for us, however, is that Hall has strongly indicated a globalization theory surpassing modernity and postmodernity. Gratitude to Hall!

We must go beyond the 'modernity' cultural studies; Hall has already made this attempt. We must go beyond the 'postmodernity' cultural studies as well, the obvious limitations of which have already been represented by Beck and Tomlinson. We need learn from both their blindness and insight and explore the possibility of a new theoretical stage.

Conclusion: Towards Global Dialogism

Globalization is internally modernity and postmodernity, that is, it simultaneously surpasses modernity and postmodernity and is therefore possible to become a new philosophical concept. Robertson's 'glocalization', Beck's 'cosmopolitanism' and Tomlinson's monographic criticism of 'cultural imperialism' are all valuable efforts to conceptualise this new era—I greatly appreciate their efforts. As a response to them, I try to make clear here my differences from them: first, I insist on the modernity perspective to globalization; I agree with Hall's insistence on contradiction and struggle; second, consequently, the postmodernity I see is modernity-postmodernity, a postmodernity that is constrained by modernity; third, inevitably, I will not see the complete disappearance of the individual and subject in postmodernity globalization. For me, the individual and the subject will just change but will not wholly give up themselves in the dialogue, in the 'inter-subjectivity' with another subject. Forth, we therefore cannot presuppose things like 'universe' beyond us as nationals or 'citizens'. As the subject cannot be eliminated, 'nation' cannot be eliminated, '*inter*-nationality' and '*inter*-locality' (Jin, 2007: 276-280) cannot be replaced by 'cosmopolitanism' or 'glocalization' with the intention of the global as a whole. In the era of globalization, every nationality or every culture has its say—we cannot decide for it what and how to say—which involves another more complicated philosophical issue: can we hold a dialogue without premise? A simple answer for this: as long as the individual cannot be totally symbolised (Lacan), ideologised (Althusser) and colonised (Spivak), we have to admit the dialogue without premise. In contemporary theories, such an idea sounds very absurd, yet for Confucius 2500 years ago, that already was a basic principle in *inter*-personal communication. Confucius does not care about the so-called 'grand' premise. He just knows to empty himself for the other to come in.

Let *other* be *other*, and let *myself* be *other* too, let both of them as limited subjects, and move 'inter-subjectivity' towards 'inter-otherness' and ontological 'inter-culturality'—only by so doing, can cultural studies in the era of globalization plan a 'dialogue' in its real sense, the consequence of which is for each interlocutor the 'incessant' self-surpassing, self-negation and self-reconstruction, 'incessant' because the interlocutor always retains his or her inner being that cannot be fully expressed, and the interlocutor on one side can never become the one on the other side no matter after how many rounds of dialogue have taken place. Metaphorically, will the leaves growing in the same tree, after hundreds years of 'dialogue', become identical with each other? Nature teaches us that human beings, in the last instance, belong to nature. They 'culturally' dialogise, while they also 'naturally' refuse dialogue, refusing 'dialogue' with 'nature'.

We will conclude with *global dialogism*, in which, first, the interlocutor as an 'other' is its foundation; second, the 'global' is not the premise of dialogue, it is not even the target, it is, nevertheless, a result that can be and/or cannot be expected, because the 'global' as such is based on the other, it is a transition from 'inter-otherness' into 'inter-subjectivity', it is mutual exploration and negotiation of the inter-subjectivity between others, during which there is no premise prior to the dialogic process designed by either side; thirdly, however, as long as the 'other' enters dialogue, it stops being the 'absolute other' because dialogue bestows the 'absolute other' a subjective dimension. The definition of 'subjectivity', as we know, is the ability to change the object and simultaneously changed by the object. By the way, one of the key meanings of 'inter-subjectivity' is the admission of the mutual changes between subjects. Back to the beginning of this essay, as *global dialogism*, globalization embraces both modernity and postmodernity, and a synthesis of which then transcends both. 'Globalization' as such is a new philosophy. If another name is needed, *global dialogism* will be a choice.

As to the question whether future cultural studies will make *global dialogism* its theoretical foundation, we cannot say yes or no, since a predetermined answer is contrary to the spirit of *global dialogism*. At the moment, what we can affirm is that in solving those serious problems arising from 'cultural imperialism' in this global age, *global dialogism* can at least simultaneously avoid 'universe' ('cosmopolitanism') and 'holism'('glocalization') dubious of supporting cultural imperialism, and total ignorance of cultural imperialism resulting from over-emphasis on the agency of the audience. Or, we may even expect to re-interpret, after Hall, the 'inter-culturality', especially its various new possibilities in the future.

Notes

1 | Hereafter all the quotations from Ulrich Beck, unless otherwise specified, are from this article which can be read as a manifesto of his theory of 'cosmopolitanism', though there is a largely extended discussion of it in his *The Cosmopolitan Vision* (Beck, 2006) that should not be neglected.

2 | Hereafter all the quotations from Rainer Winter are from this article unless otherwise specified.

3 | But Appadurai also warns that: 'This is not to suggest that consumers are free agents, living happily in a world of safe malls, free lunches, and quick fixes.' (1996: 7)

4 | In a chapter on Stuart Hall, Angela McRobbie has the saying 'structure in dominance of globalisation' (2005: 29), which is apparently a rewrite of 'a "complex structure in dominance"' coming from Hall's early essay 'Encoding/Decoding' (1981: 128). This shows that she has noticed Hall's application of his early theoretical framework in TV studies into his globalization studies.

REFERENCES

Appadurai, Arjun (1996) *Modernity at Large, Cultural Dimensions of Globalization*. Minneapolis & London: University of Minnesota Press.

Beck, Ulrich (2003) 'Rooted Cosmopolitanism: Emerging from a Rivalry of Distinctions', in Ulrich Beck, Natan Sznaider & Rainer Winter (eds.) *Global America? The Cultural Consequences of Globalization*. Liverpool: Liverpool University Press.

Beck, Ulrich (2005) *Power in the Global Age*. Trans. by Kathleen Cross. Cambridge: Polity.

Beck, Ulrich (2006) *The Cosmopolitan Vision* (Beck, 2006). Trans. by Ciaran Cronin. Cambridge: Polity.

Denzin, Norman K. (2007) 'Forward: A Cultural Studies That Matters', in Cameron McCarthy *et al.* (eds.) *Globalizing Cultural Studies: Ethnographic Interventions in Theory, Method, and Policy*. New York & Washington, D. C.: Peter Lang.

Giddens, Anthony (1990) *The Consequences of Modernity*. Stanford: Stanford University Press.

Giddens, Anthony (2002) *Runaway World, How Globalisation Is Reshaping Our Lives*. London: Profile Books.

Hall, Stuart (1973a) 'Encoding and Decoding in the Television Discourse', Stenciled Occasional Paper, CCCS, University of Birmingham.

Hall, Stuart (1973b) 'The "Structured Communication" of Events', Stenciled Occasional Paper, CCCS, University of Birmingham.

Hall, Stuart (1981 [1980]) 'Encoding/Decoding', in Stuart Hall *et al.* (eds.) *Culture, Media, Language, Working Papers in Cultural Stud-*

ies, 1972-79. London: Hutchinson, in association with CCCS, University of Birmingham.

Hall, Stuart (1991a) 'The Local and the Global: Globalization and Ethnicity', in Anthony D. King (ed.) *Culture, Globalization and the World-System, Contemporary Conditions for the Representation of Identity*. Department of Art and Art History, State University of New York at Binghamton and Macmillan Education Ltd.

Hall, Stuart (1991b) 'Old and New Identities, Old and New Ethnicities', in Anthony D. King (ed.) *Culture, Globalization and the World-System, Contemporary Conditions for the Representation of Identity*. Department of Art and Art History, State University of New York at Binghamton and Macmillan Education Ltd.

Jin, Huimin (2007) 'Redefining Global Knowledge', in *Theory, Culture and Society*. London: Sage, vol. 24, 7/8.

McCarthy, Cameron et al. (eds.) (2007) *Globalizing Cultural Studies: Ethnographic Interventions in Theory, Method, and Policy*. New York & Washington, D. C.: Peter Lang.

McRobbie, Angela (2005) 'Stuart Hall and the Inventiveness of Cultural Studies', in her own book *The Uses of Cultural Studies*. London: Sage.

Morley, Dave [David] (1974) 'Reconceptualising the Media Audience: Towards an Ethnography of Audiences', Stenciled Occasional Paper, CCCS, University of Birmingham.

Robertson, Roland (1992) *Globalization: Social Theory and Global Culture*. London: Sage.

Sznaider, Natan and Winter, Rainer (2003) 'Introduction', in Ulrich Beck, Natan Sznaider & Rainer Winter (eds.) *Global America? The Cultural Consequences of Globalization*.

Tomlinson, John (2001 [1991]) *Cultural Imperialism, A Critical Introduction*. London/New York: Continuum.

Winter, Rainer (2003) 'Global Media, Cultural Change and Transformation of the Local: The Contribution of Cultural Studies to a Sociology of Hybrid Formations', in Ulrich Beck, Natan Sznaider & Rainer Winter (eds.) *Global America? The Cultural Consequences of Globalization*.

Appendix 2. British Cultural Studies, Active Audiences and the Status of Cultural Theory

An Interview with Professor David Morley

Abstract British cultural studies, represented perhaps chiefly by the so-called Birmingham School, is much marked with its strong orientation towards the application of grounded theory in the analysis of concrete cases, rather than the development of abstract Theory with a capital T (in Stuart Hall's words). As a leading figure of the Birmingham School and a key representative of active audience model in television studies, or broadly, media studies, David Morley stands at a point where this trend was set, as is evidenced in this interview. Questioned by Huimin Jin, Morley puts his audience studies into the contexts of British cultural studies, postmodernism, Marxism, social movements, and so on; and in doing so, he shows the ambiguity, and subtlety of his concepts of how to best *theorise* the active audience. Only by this method, Jin believes, could Morley launch his version of audience studies, which aims not to invent a general theory of media effects, but to use an interdisciplinary range of theories to explore how people actually respond to a TV programme; and only by this approach to audience studies, furthermore, could Morley develop a theory of the audience' activity which is embedded in the course of their everyday life that cannot be thoroughly colonised by discourses. Cultural studies, wherever it's conducted, therefore, Morley suggests, has to construct modes of analysis which are relevant to its own conditions of production in a particular place, at a particular time. This is the tradition, as we know it, but also the future, as Morley envisages, of cultural studies.

Key Words Stuart Hall, David Morley, active audiences, British cultural studies

Huimin Jin (hereafter as HJ): To begin with, I should say thanks for your accepting my interview, Professor David Morley. As one of the leading figures of British cultural studies, represented, perhaps we could say, chiefly by the so-called Birmingham School, you should be, I believe, in a good position to clarify some issues about which I am quite curious, concerning the historical development of this school. More importantly, I am rather keen to know from your own perspective, your special contribution to British cultural studies, either in a Hall-centered mode or in a broader sense. Well, my first question is about popular culture.

Recently, scholars with Manchester Metropolitan University have shown a tendency to narrow cultural studies down to popular culture studies. By doing so, they foreground and intensify popular culture as a primary arena of cultural studies. This is related to the British tradition of cultural studies, from Williams's definition of culture as a way of life, via the CCCS subculture researches, and to the course of Popular Culture *(U203) run by the Open University from 1982 to 1987. You were invited to contribute a course unit on* Interpreting Television *for this historically significant programme. As to the ever-expanding field of popular culture studies as an academic enterprise, my concern is given to such questions as why academics should take it seriously in the British context, and if it has something specific to do with a politics of culture, say, to the* Turn to Gramsci, *or to, anthropologically, our everyday life, in which it has an enabling transformative force.*

David Morley (hereafter as DM): I see no reason at all why cultural studies should now concentrate exclusively on popular culture. Indeed, in my view, it is crucial that cultural studies also attend to middle-brow and high-brow culture, as these forms and their changing characteristics can only be understood in relation to each other. At the point of cultural studies' inception, however, the position was very different. At that moment, it was widely assumed that popular culture was not worthy of theorists' attentions. So the initial focus on popular culture was a polemical move, in a particular context, designed to show that popular culture was a field that was indeed well worth studying. However, nowadays, that point is generally accepted so it doesn't need to be stressed so much. So, to narrow cultural studies focus down to only popular culture would be a very regressive move in the contemporary situation.

You're right to point to the important shift towards perspectives derived from anthropology as a way of understanding culture as a way of life. But that argument doesn't have any specific or particular relation to the British case. It would apply, I think, to the study of culture in all societies. What is most specific to the development to cultural studies in Britain, in particular, relates to the moment of the late 1970s, and early 1980s, the moment of the 'Popular Culture' course which ran at the Open University from 1982 to 1987. That was a moment when several key factors combined, which led to the stress on the politics of popular culture. Let me explain.

At that point in the early 1980s, Mrs. Thatcher had just been elected and Stuart Hall and others argued that her victory was founded on a form of populism (rather like Ernesto Laclau argues in the case of the success of the Peronist political movement in Argentina). Hall rightly argued that Mrs. Thatcher's victory could only be understood—and effectively opposed—on the ground of culture. His point was that she had successfully articulated forms of 'authoritarian populism' which genuinely resonated with the feelings and aspirations of the dissatisfied white working class of Britain. The argument was that the core explanation for the overwhelming working class electoral vote for her was their support for her vision of the return to what she called 'traditional Victorian values'. They supported her rejection of the post-war liberal progressivism of the 1960' and 70s. Hall's argument was that, if that was so, then the understanding of the cultural dimension of politics, especially in the form of popular culture, becomes critical. At the same time, a variety of dissident groups in Britain—women, gays, black people, disabled people, etc—were also insisting there were cultural dimensions to politics. They insisted that their oppression often took cultural forms, for instance, negative stereotypes of them in jokes, or in popular entertainment and thus, they argued, the transformation of these forms of popular culture was an important dimension of political struggle. That was all part of the 'Turn to Gramsci' and that was the reason for the corresponding stress on the cultural dimension of politics, in which context, the analysis of the dynamics of popular culture was then seen as the key task.

The further point here is that you have to understand that this was an argument which was made in the face of a rather hard-line, leftist, Marxism, which said that culture was not really important at all, and attributed everything to economic factors. However, that analysis completely misses out the extent to which Mrs. Thatcher's political success worked precisely by transforming British culture—and by transforming what were understood to be British values. She had to transform those things, in order to gain the popular support to go on and win the later political and economic fights that she got into— e.g. with the miners when they went on strike for a whole year. So her *first* political victory was at the level of culture: in shifting values and reasserting the sense of individualism, individual achievement, individual ambition, and individual responsibility in all spheres of life. Having won that cultural battle, she was then in a position to win the political and economical battles. That was, in a sense, a cultural revolution in Britain: she achieved a revolution in the culture of everyday life and shifted everybody's assumptions a long way to the Right.

The long run significance of this can perhaps be seen now, after the end of the period of the 'New Labour' government. Despite the claim that New Labour had a different (and supposedly radical) approach to politics, in a very significant sense, what the New Labour government did was simply to live it out its life under the hegemony of the terms of reference established by Mrs. Thatcher. I think you could very reasonably say—as many people have done—that Tony

Blair represented Mrs. Thatcher's 'true heir', because the cultural battles that she won—about individualised responsibility, and about the free market—established the hegemony of a set of ideas which shifted the whole political terrain—and which New Labour did little to question, for fear of losing 'middle ground' electoral support. Politics in the UK today is still being fought out inside the terms of reference established by the cultural victories which Mrs. Thatcher achieved. Now the new Coalition government is pursuing that Thatcherite agenda even more radically than New Labour ever did, in its plans to totally dismantle the remnants of the Welfare State set up as part of the post-world War II settlement in the late 1940s and thus establish a new 'common sense' in which the market is taken as the hegemonic form for the modeling of all areas of social life.

HJ: There is a popular impression that your reputation in the area of cultural studies was established by your television audience researches that are mainly shown in your books The 'Nationwide' Audience *(1980),* Family Television *(1986), and then* Television, Audiences and Cultural Studies *(1992), among which the last one is more or less a theoretically retrospective interpretation of what you did in the previous two projects. From your empirical work, what theoretically, in brief, have you developed or reinforced? I should say sorry if you would think I am over-concerned with the theory per se, which may be contradictory to the tradition of British cultural studies.*

DM: It's quite true that my own reputation within cultural studies was largely founded on the audience studies that I did in the 1970s and 1980s, published as *The 'Nationwide' Audience* and *Family Television*. However, I was never in fact, particularly interested in either television or audiences themselves, as objects of study. What I was interested in was the question of cultural power. The choice to make an empirical study of television audiences was simply a way to 'operationalise' a study of the extent (and limits) of ideological or cultural hegemony, as manifested in the forms of media consumption. As for your further question, concerning what, theoretically, my empirical work has achieved, my answer would be that it has produced a far better model of the operation of media power than would have been made possible by continuing to make abstract speculations about media effects of the sort offered by such scholars as Adorno and Horkheimer in the early period, by McLuhan in the 1960s, or by Baudrillard in the postmodern version. In my view, despite the evident theoretical sophistication of much of this work, it nonetheless still operates with what is, in the end, a very simplistic motion of media effects. Even the latest version of 'new media' theory is still flawed by the simplistic assumption, carried over from Adorno and Horkheimer, that the media (or in this case, the 'new' technologies) have automatic and unavoidable 'effects' on people. Apart from anything else, that is inadequate because it is, ultimately, a technologically determinist argument. I have developed this line of critique of the severe limitations of so-called 'new media theory' most fully in the section of my last book (Morley 2007) titled 'Rhetorics of the Technological Sublime' in relation to the problems posed by the foreshortened a-historical perspective of these theories and their oversimplification of the crude binary divide which they draw between the 'old' world of the analogue media, with their audiences of supposedly passive 'couch potatoes', and the marvels of the new digital era, in which it is assumed that 'we' are all more significantly active

Clearly, my own inclination here would be to go back again to Williams' argument in *Television, Technology and Cultural Form* (2003 [1974]) which very carefully shows that technologies do *not* have effects built into them, because it's always a question of how particular technologies come to be institutionalised in particular ways. There are many social and cultural forces which act to determine that. As my own work has shown, along with that of people such as the late Roger Silverstone, new technologies don't simply have effects on people, just as media don't have direct effects on their audiences. The question is how particular people, in particular contexts, perceive the relevance (or irrelevance) of specific media technologies for their lives, and how they then choose to use those technologies—or ignore them, or indeed 'bend' them in some way, to a purpose for which they were not intended.

In either case, the effects are not directly produced. If my work has been about one thing, it has been about how to develop a more satisfactory model of the power of the media. I'm not in the business of *denying* the power of the media, or denying that particular technologies allow new things to happen. My point is to better understand *how* that power operates, in conjunction with the fact that people *do* make choices, and do make their own interpretations of material provided to them by the media, whether we are talking about the mass media of broadcasting, or the micro-mobile media of today's world.

One of the interesting points you raise in your questions is the status of 'Theory', and its position within the tradition of British cultural studies. I think it is a very interesting question and it does concern me deeply. It's very common in contemporary debates, especially among people whose background is in sociology or philosophy, rather than in cultural studies, for people to make a claim for high status by presenting themselves as 'Theorists'. However, that is an approach which, in terms of the role of theory in the tradition of cultural studies defined by Stuart Hall, can only appear as extremely naïve. Hall's version of cultural studies is not at all resistant to theory as such. But that tradition, within which I'm situated, is one in which we *use* theory in order to theorise some particular, empirically specific conjuncture or situation, *not* for the purpose of generalised and abstracted speculation. If you look at Hall's 'Marx's Notes on Method: A "Reading" of the "1857 Introduction"' (1974), the point is made very clearly there. For Hall, theory is not valued in itself, but in terms of its usefulness in *theorising* particular conjunctures. The problematic issue about philosophical-style 'Theory in the Abstract', concerns the high intellectual price which must be paid for any moment of abstraction. Of course, theoretical abstraction is a powerful, and often necessary, intellectual tool, as it allows you to condense what would otherwise be a mountain of potentially confusing data, in order to see the underlying patterns. But, just like a power-saw, it is also a potentially dangerous tool, which must be used very carefully, if it is not to do more harm than good. Of course, any abstraction or categorisation is, of its nature, reductive. The question is always whether *this* particular formal abstraction is worthwhile, in a specific case. Each time you abstract, you have to ask yourself whether the benefit you will get, in so far as the abstraction contributes to your ability to make some ordered analysis of cultural patterns, is sufficient to make up for the fact that, in making that abstraction, you'll be losing track of some part of the particularity of the situation you are trying to analyse.

Coming, as I have said, from a tradition which emphasises specificity in empirical investigations, I am unsympathetic to what the French philosopher Michel Serres (whose approach closely parallels that of Hall) calls lazy forms of 'One Size Fits All' Theory. As Serres says, it is lamentably easy to use that kind of Theory to reduce all phenomena to one ultimate set of 'truths' (whether those of Marxist economics, Semiotics, Freudian psychoanalysis, or Foucauldian discourse theory). However, as he observes, a single theoretical 'pass key' will never suffice to open all doors—rather, as he insists, each time you want to 'unlock' a specific problem, you must forge the specific theoretical key which will be adequate to the problem in hand (Serres and Latour, 1995).

I'm interested in 'grounded' forms of theory. So, for example, if we take the case of TV as a medium, I would not want to say that Television is (essentially) a thing which has some particular set of facets—or that it is in the *'essence'* of the medium, philosophically understood, that it should *always* have these effects. Rather than that very deterministic and mechanical mode of analysis, I'm interested in understanding how things work in particular circumstances or contexts, when media technologies are actually used by different people.

Of course, we must find a way to see the deep-seated (and sometimes hidden) patterns in our data and it is no good disavowing all generalisations and ending up in a poststructuralist morass of just telling a million individual stories of infinite difference. But we must, nonetheless, use those generalisations very cautiously and be attentive to the extent to which, every time we make a generalisation, we pay a price, in the loss of contextual specificity. The question is one of always keeping one's eyes on the 'price ticket'—making sure that what you lose in the use of that theoretical abstraction is outweighed by the gains in analytical power that it enables.

HJ: When you were developing your theory of active audiences, did you have in mind German reception-theory such as the works of the Konstanz School, say, Hans Herbert Jauss and Wolfgang Iser? Or, you might have had some other theoretical resources available? It looks as if British cultural studies concurs basically with reception-theory in assuming that audiences are never passive receivers of media messages, or that, furthermore, the reception or consumption of television messages can be elevated as a part of the whole television production.

DM: Your question puts me in mind of the story that Janice A. Radway tells in the introduction to the British edition of her book *Reading the Romance* (1987 [1984]), which was published here some years after its initial publication in America. There, Radway explains that, when she subsequently discovered British cultural studies work (including my own work on television audiences) she was astounded to discover how closely it 'fitted' with the perspective that she, independently, had been developing in her ethnographic work on women readers of romance fiction.

The situation was rather parallel, I think, in terms of my own relation to the German theories to which you refer. In fact, I only came across the work of Jauss and Iser at some point in the early 1980's, well after my work on the *'Nationwide' Audience* had been done. What was interesting, of course, was that, rather like Radway, I then had the experience of coming across a body of fascinating theoretical work which was very close to what I had been doing, even though it wasn't directly influential in the construction of my own perspective. This is perhaps a general point about the fact that, if something is a good idea, it is probably going to be worked out by more than one person, in more than one place, often simultaneously! So Jauss and

Iser and I end up, not exactly in the same place, but on relatively close theoretical paths, although we got there from different routes, and by means of different theoretical resources.

In terms of my own theoretical resources, the key ones were socio-linguistics and cultural anthropology. I believe I was the first person to use the now well-worn term 'ethnography' in relation to media audiences, in a paper that I wrote in 1972 'Reconceptualising the Media Audience: Towards an Ethnography of Audiences' (1974). Where did I get that from? From the work of people Dell Hymes and Clifford Geertz in cultural anthropology. As for the resources used to analyse the interpretations which people made of television programmes (which was the key main in the *'Nationwide' Audience* study), the key elements came from debates in the sociology of education about the role of linguistic codes in determining children's educational success or failure—which was a theory which seemed to me to also be applicable to how the availability of different cultural resources might play some part in determining patterns of decoding TV. At that time, in Britain in the early 1970s, the key debate was between Basil Bernstein and his critic Harold Rosen. The issue at stake was to do with the role of class structure in the determination of language abilities and language uses. Bernstein had a rather deterministic approach, which was very important in identifying differences between working class language and middle class language, much of which has very close parallels with the work of Pierre Bourdieu in France about the social distribution of cultural capital and cultural competencies. Conversely, while Rosen appreciated of the power of those analyses, he was very concerned that they were being conducted in too essentialist a way. Rosen was aware that while class (or gender, or racial origin, or the membership of any kind of social category) is very likely to have some effect on the forms of cultural capital to which someone in a given social position has access, this is not an *automatic* process. He was also concerned with the way which people 'inhabit' their membership of any particular collectivity. In a certain sense, already, in the 1970s Rosen was making exactly the kind of argument which someone like Judith Butler makes now, 30 years later. Just as Butler says that we are not all living in what she calls the 'prison house of gender' (because there are different ways of inhabiting the category of masculinity or femininity), Rosen is making the same point about class: we are not just 'prisoners' of class—because there are different ways of inhabiting middle class or working class identities. The main problem with Bernstein's model is that it just avoided this issue entirely in its sociological determinism, assuming that the effects of class position were more or less automatic. This is a criticism which some of us would say also applies to the work of Bourdieu—which has much in common with that of Bernstein. Thus, one could make an analogy and say that if Bernstein was the English version of Bourdieu, his critic, Rosen, was the equivalent of Michel de Certeau, one of Bourdieu's most important critics in France.

So, to go back to where I started in my answer to this question, my main theoretical resources came from cultural anthropology, in terms of providing a model for a 'close reading' of particular actions as understood in context. They also came from sociolinguistics—and especially from Vološinov's insistence on the 'multi-accentuality' of the sign, his insistence (in contradiction of Saussure) that there is no totally shared language system (Saussure's *'langue'*) in a given society, and that one has to be sensitive to the conflicts that are fought out in and through language and culture.

HJ: If you hold that 'individual readings will be framed by shared cultural formations and practices preexistent to the individual' (Morley, 1980: 15), though in a complex and subtle way, how could you demarcate your theory of active, therefore, resistant audiences from the Frankfurt School's 'non-resistant' conception of the masses that are passively injected with a prevailing ideology? When the masses begin to decode the televisional texts, they might have been 'pre-mass-ed' by some other factors—social or ideological, which you admit as preexistent, other than by the modern communications, television included—by ideology, or precisely, being part of ideological totality or ideological apparatuses, a role, whatever it may be, which you seem to hesitate to recognise. To be clear, my inference here is that so long as you assert that individual interpretations are socially, at least partially, determined, you would have already accepted that the cultural industry *as a social or ideological force and apparatus does play a role in making the* masses. *This argument may be supported by the text's role to which you still attach importance: Interpretations are not 'arbitrary' but 'subject to constraints contained within the text itself'* (Morley, 1980: 148-49).

DM: Essentially, in the *'Nationwide' Audience* I was trying to offer what I think is a better way of understanding media power than is offered by the Frankfurt School's simplistic approach to audiences—as passive 'dupes'—which was predominant at that time. I'm quite happy to accept that Adorno and Horkheimer make sophisticated *general* arguments about the way in which the culture industry shapes consciousness. In criticising their model of the *automatic* 'effects' of the media on the masses, I'm not trying to replace it by a theory which says that all audiences are completely 'active' and are making just any interpretation they want out of the media materials they come across. In that respect, my perspective is quite different from that of scholars such as John Fiske in what has come to be called the 'active audiences' tradition. Contrary to them, I'm not trying to deny issues of media power. Moreover, despite my criticisms of Bourdieu and Bernstein's overly deterministic model of class, I'm also very interested in the way in which the ability of a person to re-interpret or re-use the media to which they have access is, in fact, *to some extent* determined by their social position. That's because their social position will limit their access to particular types of cultural codes and cultural capital. However, I'm *not* advocating some model of 'free-floating' individuals who are just able to do whatever they like with what the media offer to them.

Here I would also distinguish my own position from that of people like Ulrich Beck: when Beck says that in today's 'individualised' world, class is no more than a 'zombie' category of little use in analysing social life, I think he is quite wrong. Class continues to exercise profound effects on people's lives—especially in an era where, in the UK at least, rates of inter-generational mobility are declining:

so that class position at birth is now an even *better* predictor of an individual's probable life course than it was 30 years ago. Of course, class or any other mode of social categorisation (such as gender or ethnicity) can be used in an overly deterministic—and thus, 'zombie-like' way—but that is a matter of how exactly you use the categories in your analysis, not whether or not the categories are intrinsically useful or not.

I'm also quite prepared to accept that the socio-cultural 'identities' which I use in the *'Nationwide' Audience* analysis as *explanations* of how this or that person interprets of particular programme, are themselves socially and culturally constructed. In English, we have this expression, which is a kind of rhetorical figure, or joke, in which one says: 'which came first, the chicken or the egg'? In one way it is just a silly joke. But, at another level, it expresses a rather profound philosophical dilemma. Of course, in a sense, it doesn't matter which came first. What you have to understand is what their relationship is. The same goes for the question of the role of the culture industry in the construction of consciousness and in the provision of the materials out of which people construct their identities, through the decoding of TV programmes, among other things. The subsequent issue is how you can then look at those identities themselves as partly explaining why this person, in this particular position, will tend to be affected (or not affected) by these particular media, or how they will tend to interpret some particular media programme. One has to understand that as a dialectical process between determination and activity: to go back to the original, as Marx says, men and women make their history, but not in conditions of their own choice.

In the media field, what we are looking at is the way in which social positions go some way to determining the cultural resources available to you, the cultural choices you can make—out of which you construct your identity. Now that's not to say that you construct your identity on a *'tabula rasa'* in a world of completely free choices—that you could decide to just be anybody, or do anything at random, or interpret the media just any way you like—you couldn't. We all have only a certain limited repertoire of possibilities available to us, and yet nonetheless, within that circumscribed repertoire, there are still choices to be made, and those choices are significant. One can't explain the determination as total or automatic—to take that view is just to wipe out the complexity of the dialectic which is at the heart of the process.

HJ: *Adapting from Frank Parkin, Stuart Hall (1973) argues that there may be three 'hypothetical' positions from which a media message is decoded by audiences: the dominant-hegemonic, the negotiated, and the oppositional, among which the latter two, compared with the first, which rarely happens in reality, are stressed for their frequency. It can be seen that there is a point at which your theory of active audiences encounters this argument: the resistance implicit in all interpretations of media texts. Here my concern is with the questions that what makes a reading active or resistant, and why the cultural industry is not able to knead all the receivers simply into the masses.*

DM: I agree with the proposition, implicit in your question, that in a sense, *all* readings are active. To make any sense at all of a TV message you firstly, have to interpret the dots and noise on the screen as representing images of people, or voices and so on, and you've got to read the rules of perspective, through which you can reconstruct the image of a three-dimensional world from a two-dimensional screen. Thus, activity is always present in the interpretation of media messages. As for when an interpretation is resistant, that is quite a difficult question. You could argue, for instance, that in the '*Nationwide*' *Audience*, the reaction of the young black students who dismiss '*Nationwide*' as irrelevant to them, and who refuse, in a sense, to make any decoding of it at all, is far more radical a move than that of the left wing trade unionists in the study, who produce a classically oppositional reading of the '*Nationwide*' text, but who do so from *within* a framework in which they recognise the programme as relevant to them. While accepting some of the political terms in play, they make a critical counter-argument to them, and that is a form of opposition, certainly. But you could argue that the reaction of those who dismiss the whole genre of that kind of politics as irrelevant to them (as the young black students do) is, in another sense, a much *more* radical form of negativity, and I don't think that Parkin's model is able to deal with that question. That model (and the way Hall initially takes it up) rather assumes that consciously politicised opposition is the most active, and most radical, and in that sense, the most important form of response to the media. I'm not sure that it is the case and that's why, as my work developed, I begin to 'operationalise' the model in a slightly different way, so as to take account of the ways in which all readings are active (whether the dominant, negotiated or oppositional modes of decoding), but also to take account of the fact that the forms of activity are themselves various, in ways which Parkin's model is not really capable of dealing with.

HJ: Social-contextually, why did the Frankfurt School choose a passive model of media consumers while British cultural studies an active one? To put it differently, what are the social conditions that underlie this shift of media studies, if there are any that work? In connection with this, textually, I doubt that mass culture *and* popular culture *are referred by them to the same media texts and/or in the same way, even though they might overlap. I wonder if categorically the* masses *are more closely associated with the* producers *of the cultural industry while the* popular *more with* consumers *of the products. If it is true, can we argue that this shift reflects a social transformation from production society to consumer society, as Jean Baudrillard has distinguished them, and that your audience theory is rooted in such a consumer society in which people have more choices, in the face of a plethora of commodities?*

DM: I think I'd put it rather differently! I'm not sure that you can understand the Frankfurt School's model of media power without thinking quite specifically of the contexts of Weimar and Nazi Germany in the 1930's, when those theories were being developed. There you have the context of the emergence of powerful new media—in that case, radio and cinema—and new forms of political rhetoric, operating in a relation to a population which, in its mobility from rural to urban areas, was becoming '*anomic*' and thus more vulnerable to persuasion and propaganda. Those circumstances demand attention and sensitivity to questions of media power and manipulation. That is why Adorno and Horkheimer were interested in the particular questions that they focus on. British cultural studies certainly arises in very different circumstances, but I'm not sure that I would interpret that in the way that you seem to imply, in your question.

As I understand your argument, you are suggesting that we face a move from a 'producer society' to a 'consumer society', that the concept of 'the masses' (as mobilised in the Frankfurt School's work) is a characteristic of a what you call a producer society—and that popular culture is then, conversely, associated with the consumer society. From that premise, if I understand you rightly, you see 'active audience theory' as being to do with the extent to which, in this thing called the 'consumer society', people have more choices.

I think that's a problematic form of historical periodisation and one which is characteristic of a certain type of sociological approach—many social theorists love inventing new periodisations! For example, nowadays many are people talking about Deleuze and something called '*The* control society', without a clear definition of what that is or when (and where) it started! Then people speak of '*The* consumer society': but that has various definitions. You could talk about the consumer society of post-war Europe in the 1950s, or you could talk about today's emerging consumer society in China, which seems to me to operate in very different kind of way. Those would, minimally, have to be understood as rather different sub-types of the overall concept: and once you recognise that, it follows that you cannot just assume that the same tendencies will apply in the same ways, in these different contexts.

Rather than thinking in terms of a total shift in historical periods, from producer to consumer society, as you suggest (a shift in which power is understood to have moved from the producers to the consumers), my own perspective would be to say that in *both* situations, there always have been—and still are—*both* aspects of that question. That is to say, in what you would refer to as the 'producer society' of the era of mass culture, there were still choices to be made. People still did choose between this or that aspect of mass culture and indeed, reacted to it, or interpreted it, in different ways—so they were still active, even then. And conversely, even now, in this so-called consumer society, where people do get to make more choices, we mustn't confuse choice with empowerment in any simple sense, nor with a loss of producer power. I might have a larger number of channels from which to choose what to watch on my television set these days, but it's still a menu set by someone else, within which I have to choose.

To put it another way, I'm more interested in the continuities and crossovers between these so-called different 'periods' or different 'types' of society than I am in just accepting such clear binary divisions unproblematically. In that respect I'm influenced by Derrida's insistence on deconstructing and destabilising those kind of binaries—and by his insistence on the need to pay attention to the ambivalences which cut across the kind of binary divisions of which sociologists, in particular, are rather too fond of for my liking!

HJ: Did the postmodernism, for instance, of Fredric Jameson, Michel Foucault, Roland Barthes and Jean Baudrillard (in any other aspects, rather than his social periodisation which you quite suspect) help to shape your television studies, and in the first place, of course, your audience studies? If so, in what ways did it work? You know, postmodern declarations such as the death of author, or of subjectivity, were quite provocative and they tend to emphasise the role of readers in the process of reception.

DM: Let me take those authors in stages. Barthes was certainly influential for me, at an early stage, in setting up the kind of semiological model with which I was working. But I rapidly moved towards Vološinov's critique of that rather rigid form of semiology. (Here one must also note that, later in his career, Barthes himself became skeptical of his early dream of a 'scientific semiology'!) So Barthes' was influential, but perhaps Umberto Eco more so, especially in his essay 'Does the Audience Have Bad Effects on Television?' (1995 [1994]).

But Vološinov was the key resource, in producing an analysis that was attentive to the mobility of signs; to the conflict between signs; to what he calls the multi-accentuality of signs; and to the way in which different people will use the same sign or word or image for very different purposes.

As for postmodernism, the story is rather different. The simple fact is that postmodernism came much later—Baudrillard, Jameson and Foucault only came to have influence in cultural studies circles in the U.K. long after I produced the *'Nationwide'* and *Family Television* studies. Again, as far as these periodisations go, just as I'm not much enamoured of the notion of mass society, or consumer society, or production society, or control society, likewise 'Postmodernity' seems to me a rather weakly defined category. The notion that ours simply 'is' a postmodernism era, seems problematic to me, unless I know when it began, which in turn, all depends on which definition of modernity or modernism you are using. If there is such a thing as a postmodern era, it's hard to imagine that it started on the same day and exists in the same form in Tokyo, Los Angeles or in some village in rural Uganda.

Overall, I'm more interested in the notion of how differential temporalities often coexist in any one historical moment. In this respect I'm influenced by historians of the Annales School, such as Fernand Braudel, and his ideas of differential historical time or, at a simpler level, Raymond Williams' notion of the coexistence of 'emergent' and 'residual' dimensions in a culture, alongside whatever is 'dominant' at that particular time. In that context, one interesting issue, it seems to me, is to do with the different sequences in which particular theorists are read in different cultural contexts. What I have in mind here is how all of this might possibly seem to you, and to a Chinese audience, reading about these things in the 21st century, 25 years or so after I was principally involved in doing this kind of work on TV audiences, in a quite different context.

Let me put that point another way. In a public debate at a conference, I was once asked what the difference was between British cultural studies and American cultural studies, and I had to come up with an instant answer! In that setting, my answer was that it was the difference between Foucault read through Gramsci, and Gramsci read through Foucault. The point is that, in Britain, people had been reading Gramsci in cultural studies, and then discovered Foucault, and began to rethink Gramsci a little bit, in terms of what difference Foucault's intervention made to that perspective. Conversely, in America, a lot of people in cultural studies came across Foucault first and only came to Gramsci subsequently, at the moment when British cultural studies 'imported' Gramsci into the USA. So what you get in much American cultural studies is a framework that is fundamentally Foucauldian, but which then works in a little bit of Gramsci. My point is that this difference of sequence, in terms of theoretical influences, has considerable significance. One has to pay attention to the modes of cultural transmission, and be sensitive to the complex routes through which particular theories come to dominance in different circumstances. One mustn't presume that which is, or was, useful or significant at one moment in a particular place, will work in the same way, or have the same significance in a different set of circumstances.

Let me give you another example, I once did some work with the late Italian semiologist Mauro Wolf, who died a few years ago. Before his death, he was working on a book in which he was going to translate George Gerbner's works on 'cultivation analysis' into Italian, in order to develop a model of the long term effects of the Italian media. What was interesting about this was the potential significance of Gerbner' work in Italy at that particular moment in the very early 1990's. As far as people in the British or American cultural studies tradition were concerned, by then, Gerbner's work seemed rather old fashioned—and very much 'displaced' by the work in Italian semiotics of people like Eco. However, Wolf could see that if you *started* from semiological premises, as Italian media scholars naturally did given the strength of that tradition's development in Italy, then importing Gerbner into the debate at *that* point could prove very useful. I'm making an elementary point about the way in which the significance of any particular theory or theorist may vary immensely according to its context in different times and different places, and according to the very different sequences in which intellectual life develops in particular countries.

As for the question of the 'death of the author', and the 'birth of the reader', again, rather like what I said in relation to your counter-position of 'producer society' and 'consumer society' (and in relation to any notion that should be understood to just move directly from the one to the other), I don't think that you have to 'kill' the author in order to give birth to the reader! I think we still have to think about *both* authors and readers. I quite agree with the polemical thrust of Barthes' original proposition, that we have to find a way to allow more space to the reader than was allowed by classical literary theory. But I don't believe that, in order to do that, we need to get rid of the idea of authorship, not least because texts do still have authors, even if those authors are now sometimes collective agents (e.g. film crews) rather than solitary individuals.

To give you a different example, there's a wonderful moment where, in his debate with John Searle, Derrida (an author who is often assumed to oppose any idea of fixed textual meaning) claims his authority over his own texts very strongly. Thus, there's a moment in which he criticises John Searle for having 'misread' of one of his texts. And Derrida says: 'As the author, I claim the authority to tell Searle what I meant.' So there you have Derrida, the *doyen* of deconstructionism, claiming authority by virtue of authorship. That perhaps indicates that authors are not yet quite dead, and indeed, they don't *need* to be dead in order for readers to breathe.

HJ: Don't you think the ways in which television programmes are structured, or rather, de-structured, are postmodern-styled? You know, in his article 'Cleverness is All,' which you quoted to deal with the topic of postmodernism, M. Ignatieff finds that in television programmes, narrative is replaced by flow, connection by disconnection and sequence by randomness (quoted in Morley, 1996: 61). Besides, as you noticed, Dick Hebdige also points to the characteristics of such texts: 'Popular culture offers a rich iconography, a set of symbols, objects and artifacts, which can be assem-

bled and reassembled by different groups in a literally limitless number of combinations.' (Dick Hebdige, 1979: 104) My further question is then that if this new kind of text, appearing first and foremost in television programmes, was a driving force, among others, that helped to open your horizon of active audiences.

DM: No, my analysis was developed in the mid-1970s, long before this notion of postmodern 'flow', disconnection, or randomisation really had much significance in the world of the media. The media I was analysing, both in the *'Nationwide'* project and in the *Family Television* project were fairly conventional forms of narrative, and were characterised neither by disconnection or randomness. But, beyond that point, I have some conceptual problems with the question. Firstly, I'm not convinced by the generalisation that television (or 'the media') are 'nowadays' more disconnected and random than they were at some earlier moment. I'm not sure how powerful that proposition is. It may be true at a high level of abstraction, but there really isn't very much which is true about 'Television in General'. So, from my point of view, as I explained earlier, it's difficult to contrast the 'television of today' with the 'television of yesterday' unless you fill in at least some of the gaps and say *which* television, *where*? Otherwise, the generalisation is so large as to hide rather more than it reveals. Indeed, one might well argue that there has always been much more variation *within* television at any given moment than there is between the television of one era and the television of another.

Secondly, I don't think that audience activity depends on disconnection; people can be very active with very closed texts. Umberto Eco is very interesting about the contradictions that one can see play, in that situation, in relation to the manipulation of 'closed' texts. I also think there is an interesting question to do with historical development. In the 1970s, you get a very important moment when structuralist analysts criticise the traditional forms of content analysis, insisting that you cannot understand a television programme by simply counting the disaggregated bits, in the way that traditional content analysis does. Their argument is that a programme is a structured whole, and so you can only understand the meaning of one bit of content *in relation to* the other bits with which they are combined. That analysis, first developed in film theory was then largely taken over from film to television studies, so then, many scholars stopped doing the traditional kinds of content analysis of television, because they understand that they needed to look holistically at the whole structure of a programme.

But then, a further difficulty came with the ethnographic evidence that gradually accumulated, showing that's *not* how people watch television, especially once you have conveniences such as the automatic control device—with which a person can change channels without moving, by simply flicking a button. What you begin to get then is a new mode of viewing, in which people don't necessarily sit down and watch *whole* TV programmes. In fact, most people, most of the time, only consume *bits* of different television programmes—they might go out to do something else in the middle, they might change programmes and watch something else and then come back later to the one they started with. At that point, the structuralist critique of content analysis loses its force. One has to recognise that, in so far as viewing modes are increasingly fragmented, it might be the case that the kind of 'cumulative effects' of media patterns of images and statements, of the type researched by Gerbner, might have more relevance than the structuralist critics of the 1970s have supposed, precisely because that critique was premised on the audience displaying a mode of focused attention on the complete, single text. That premise may be feasible if your object of study is film, shown in special places called cinemas—but it is not feasible when applied to the study, for instance, of domestic television, where the circumstances generally dictate a rather different, more distracted, mode of consumption. However, one still has to allow for certain exceptions. There are moments, even in contemporary conditions of domestic consumption, in which someone might well sit down and watch a whole text—e.g. of their 'favourite' programme. Conversely, there may be occasions in which someone goes to the cinema and, for whatever reason, doesn't concentrate on the film all the way through. You can't *presume* a 1:1 relationship between a particular architecture of display and a particular mode of consumption. Nor can you presume that there is only one mode of consumption for one particular medium. One can realistically, and usefully, only research the identifiable patterns of consumption of different media in different contexts, and one must always be sensitive to variations of the sorts I have indicated.

HJ: In the field of popular culture studies, how has British cultural studies responded to French poststructuralism, or broadly, to postmodernism? Would you please give me an overview of their interactions or contestations in interpreting popular culture? It seems to me that British cultural studies has never given up its modernist perspective by which popular culture is not depthless, superficial, and then meaningless as Fredric Jameson claims, but a site of ideological struggles, negotiations, concessions, compromises, or in short, of exactly that meaningfulness.

DM: My own position is that, interesting and stimulating as both Jameson and Baudrillard can be, there is something fundamentally elitist about the contempt in which they both hold popular culture and thus, about the contempt in which they implicitly also hold the majority of the people who are engaged with popular culture. To dismiss this whole field as depthless, superficial, and meaningless, as they do, seems to me an act of the most stunning arrogance and that is definitely not a direction which I'd want to follow. I notice that, in a previous question, you referred approvingly, to the work of Hebdige. I think that, by contrast to people like Jameson and Baudrillard, he is an elegant example of some would never make the mistake of dismissing popular culture as ei depthless, superficial or meaningless. Rather like Hebdige, my ern is to understand the forms and modalities of but in doing so, I take very seriously the meanings at stake for its p. To go back to one of my answers to an earlier question, I think it would be impossible to understand the rise of Thatcherism in Britain without understanding how that battle was fought out on field of popular culture. I don't think that was in the slightest bit 'meaningless'. I do also think there was a difference between what one could see 'on the surface' and the hidden significances that one could read, at deeper level, from the visible, 'symptomatic' events. Some of the things that might have *seemed* rather superficial, in fact, turned out to be of huge cultural, economic and political significance, and it was only by studying these seemingly trivial shifts in popular culture very carefully that it was possible to establish what was happening in Britain culture and politics in that period. The same would follow now: one needs to analyse the contemporary developments of popular culture with the same degree of seriousness—a theoretical point which goes back, beyond Stuart Hall, to Richard Hoggart's early work on popular culture in the UK in the 1950s.

HJ: *There is an argument which says that the good days of British cultural studies are now long past. It might be true to the extent that Stuart Hall has been retired for years and the CCCS has been closed, and that, what is more critical, there have been few new themes and core figures emerging that generate as much interest as broadly as before. However, from another point of view, after these changes, it is time for us to redefine, with some critical reflections, British cultural studies or cultural studies. There are many other centers for cultural studies both in and outside Britain, i.e., cultural studies becomes increasingly international. Concerning the new context, I am quite interested in questions such as how British cultural studies is going on in Britain, in what way you and your colleagues continue British cultural studies, how we can promote cultural studies in a global sense, and last, back to our main topic in this interview, how you think about popular culture that crosses boundaries: popular culture is always not only domestically but also globally popular.*

DM: Clearly, this is a very difficult and important issue. The story of the influence, internationally, of British cultural studies, is perhaps best understood as a kind of 'export industry' through which a particular set of perspectives, initially developed in Britain in the 1960s and 70s, addressing the specific problems of British society, were gradually exported to the English-speaking territories of the previous British empire, most notably Australia, Canada and then at a later point, to America. Manifestly, British cultural studies was designed to analyse the situation of a particular country at a particular time. Of course, there are certain theoretical and analytical positions built into it which can be abstracted and transported to different circumstances, allowing for the relevant variations and distinctions that need to be made. However, the idea that British cultural studies can usefully be exported as a kind of 'ready made' template, according to which the whole world can be understood, is clearly nonsensical: that would just be another form of cultural imperialism, this time, in the intellectual sphere. Cultural studies, wherever it's conducted, has to construct modes of analysis which are relevant to its own conditions of production in a particular place, at a particular time.

For instance, it may well be that someone trying to develop a cultural studies perspective in China now, as I understand you are doing, can hope to learn certain things from the history of the development of cultural studies in Britain, or elsewhere. But you have to approach those previous intellectual traditions, located elsewhere, with a strong element of critical intelligence and you have to think carefully about in what ways, given the many differences between British and Chinese society, you would need to transpose the modes of analysis developed in Britain, in order for them to be any use at all in China. So again, that takes us back to the contextual specificity of cultural studies.

One also has to be attentive to the way which the world around us has changed significantly since the 1970s when my own audience work was actually conducted. The model of cultural studies that we developed in Britain then was one which was premised on the notion of a *national* society. We were primarily concerned with class, race and gender differences within Britain, and with the British media. Certainly, those still remain very important problems but nowadays, communications is simply not national in the way that it was in the 1970s. We now have transnational broadcast systems, and satellite systems of communication, which mean that messages are mobile, all over the place. Cultures are no longer simply national. That is the force of Appadurai's argument about 'difference and disjuncture' (1996: 27ff) in the global economy, when he talks about how the 'mediascapes' of the contemporary world now exceed national boundaries. He also talks there about how the 'ethnoscapes'of our contemporary situation also now transcend national boundaries, in so far as we live in a situation in which not only are messages mobile across boundaries, but so too, are audiences. In a world of increased migrancy, we are now in a situation, as he says, where 'moving messages meet deterritorialised viewers' (1996: 4).

Now, clearly, that is a very different situation from the one that we faced in Birmingham in 1972, when I began my studies of audiences—and we have to allow for those differences in any contemporary analysis that we want to make. At the same time, to go back to what I said before about my anxiety about clearly 'binarised' divisions and periodisations, I don't want to suggest that the age of the nation state or 'the national era' is completely over—or that we now all live in some 'transnational' period, in which we are all equally mobile and all attending to messages which come to us from far away. That's simply not the case. Some people, in some places, are much more transnational than others, and many still effectively live out their lives within both national—and even more local—boundaries. That was the problem that I explored in my book *Home Territories* (2000), which was focused on questions of mobility and the media, but was also insistent on continuing to pay attention to the ways in which boundaries of a local, regional or national kind, are still, in many ways, enforced today. Indeed, it would seem to me that in China, in particular, the nation state is not only 'still alive' but is both thriving and powerful, if in different ways than within the nations of Europe.

In ending, let me say again that we clearly cannot take any mode of analysis, be it British cultural studies or anything else, and imagine that it will automatically help us understand the situation in another culture at a different time, without making all manner of cultural translations and transpositions. However, on the other hand, we have no need to imagine that we live in some totally 'new' world, where all previous theories are now redundant. As people like Carolyn Marvin (1990[1988]) have shown us, *all* technologies, all media, were new in their own time: the telegraph, the cinema, the radio, the television, the video game, the computer (cf. Morley, 2007: 243). There is always a moral panic about the latest 'new' medium and its supposed 'effects' and many of the problems we face today have clear historical precedents which we need to consider. I think that we have to develop a much more serious historical and comparative set of perspectives within cultural studies. And I hope that you and your colleagues in China will find some parts of what I have to say in this interview of use to you in your project of trying to do that! Thank you.

REFERENCES

Appadurai, Arjun (1996) *Modernity at Large: Cultural Dimensions of Globalization*. Minneapolis & London: University of Minnesota Press.

Eco, Umberto (1995 [1994]) 'Does the Audience have Bad Effects on Television?', in Umberto Eco, *Apocalypse Postponed*, ed. & trans. by Robert Lumley. London: Flamingo.

Hall, Stuart (1974) 'Marx's Notes on Method: A "Reading" of the "1857 Introduction"', *Working Papers in Cultural Studies* 6, Birmingham: University of Birmingham.

Hall, Stuart (1973) 'Encoding and Decoding in the Television Discourse'. Stenciled Occasional Paper, CCCS, University of Birmingham.

Hebdige, Dick (1979) *Subculture: The Meaning of Style*. London: Methuen.

Marvin, Carolyn (1988) *When Old Technologies Were New: Thinking about Communication in the Late Nineteenth Century*. New York: Oxford University Press.

Morley, Dave (1974) 'Reconceptualising the Media Audience: Towards an Ethnography of Audiences'. Stenciled Occasional Paper, CCCS, University of Birmingham.

Morley, David (1980) *The 'Nationwide' Audience: Structure and Decoding*. London: British Film Institute.

Morley, David (1986) *Family Television: Cultural Power and Domestic Leisure*. London: Comedia.

Morley, David (1992) *Television, Audiences and Cultural Studies*. London & New York: Routledge.

Morley, David (1996) 'Postmodernism: The Rough Guide', in James Curran, David Morley and Valerie Walkerdine (eds.) *Cultural Studies and Communications*. London: Arnold.

Morley, David (2000) *Home Territories: Media, Mobility and Identity*. London & New York: Routledge.

Morley, David (2007) *Media, Modernity and Technology: The Geography of the New*. London & New York: Routledge.

Radway, Janice A. (1987 [1984]) *Reading the Romance*. London: Verso.

Serres, Micel and Latour, Bruno (1995) *Conversations on Science, Culture and Time*. Ann Arbor: University of Michigan Press

Vološinov, V. N. (1986) *Marxism and Philosophy of Language*, trans. Ladislav Matejka and I. R. Titunik. Cambridge, Massachusetts & London: Harvard University Press.

Williams, Raymond (2003 [1974]) *Television, Technology and Cultural Form*, ed. by Ederyn Williams with a new preface by Roger Silverstone. London & New York: Routledge.

ACKNOWLEDGEMENTS

This interview, suggested by Stuart Hall, was started on Dec. 13, 2005 when I visited Prof. David Morley in his Goldsmith office. The interview text was transcribed from the tapes first by Mr. Guanxi Chen, Capital Normal University, and then by Dr. Daojian Zhang, Beijing Language & Culture University. I am very much indebted to their hard but effective work. The transcribed draft was edited and reviewed for publication by Prof. Morley around the turn of 2009 and 2010. Last but not least, my heartfelt thanks are due to the British Academy which approved my research proposal on British cultural studies and generously awarded me a fellowship which made, among others, this interview possible.

About the Author

Huimin Jin is 211 Chair Professor of Cultural Theory & Aesthetics at Shanghai International Studies University, Shanghai, and Professor of Literary Theory at the Chinese Academy of Social Sciences, Beijing. He also teaches regularly at Henan University, Kaifeng and Shaanxi Normal University, Xi'an. His publications in Chinese, among others, include *Post-Confucian Turn* (2008), *Consequences of New Media: A Critical Theory Concerning the End of Literature* (2005), *Postmodernity and Dialectical Hermeneutics* (2002), *Beyond the Will: A Study of Arthur Schopenhauer's Philosophy and Aesthetics* (1999 & 2007), and *Anti-Metaphysics and Contemporary Aesthetics* (1997). He has published several articles in English, among which, the most important one is 'Simulacrum: An Aesthetization or An-esthetization' (*Theory, Culture & Society*, London: Sage, vol. 25, no. 6, 2008). He is Editor of the journal *Difference* (Kaifeng: Henan University Press).

Index

Absolute Spirit 98
Adorno, T. 34-35, 150, 156, 160
aesthetics 138
Althusser, L. 19, 43-44, 51-54, 58-77, 80, 89-90, 98, 100, 112, 135-137, 140
American new historicism 88
Americanization 127-128, 130-131, 133
Anderson, B. 85
Anderson, P. 64, 69
Ang, I. 22, 98, 100-102, 107
Annales School 162
Appadurai, A. 131, 141-142, 171
articulation 33, 43, 54, 67, 72-73, 122-123
authoritarian populism 147

Barker, C. 16
Barthes, R. 89, 161, 164
Batsleer, J. 48
Baudrillard, J. 34-36, 150, 159, 161-162, 167
Beck, U. 127-130, 132-133, 139, 141-143, 156
Bernstein, B. 154-155
Bernstein, J. M. 35

Biemel, W. 111
Birmingham School 13, 16, 17, 23, 145-146
Bourdieu, P. 154-156
Braudel, F. 162
British cultural studies 15-17, 19, 23-27, 29, 45, 47-48, 68, 98, 100, 134-137, 145-146, 149, 151, 153, 159-160, 162-163, 167-170, 172
Butler, J. 154

Carr, E. H. 88
Chambers, I. 88-90
Chen, K.-H. 23
cognitive mapping 16-17
communicative action 103
concrete individual 52-53, 58, 67, 71, 73, 84, 98
concrete subject 52, 67, 71, 98
Confucius 102-104, 124, 140
consumer society 123, 159-162, 164
contextualism 96, 102
Copernicus 69-70
cosmopolitanism 127-130, 132, 139, 141-142

creolization 138
Cronin, C. 142
Cross, K. 142
Cubitt, S. 97
cultural dupe 40
cultural imperialism 20-21, 76-77, 119-120, 124-133, 135-139, 141, 143, 169
cultural materialism 93, 112
Cultural Revolution 116
cultural unconscious 65, 108, 114
culturalism 24
culture industry 16-18, 34-35, 84, 98, 131, 134, 137, 156-157
Curran, J. 172

Davies, T. 48
de Certeau, M. 155
encoding/decoding 17, 24, 29-30, 32, 39, 41, 44-48, 54-55, 59-60, 136, 142
deconstruction 126, 134, 136, 164
deconstructionism 164
Denzin, N. K. 124, 142
Derrida, J. 16, 55, 58, 61, 74, 122, 126, 130, 133, 161, 164
determinism 69-70, 72, 75-76, 85, 155
diaspora 138
discursive subject 29, 36, 38-39, 51, 53, 75
Du, Fu 14-15
During, S. 16, 39, 40-41

Eagleton, T. 19, 90-91
Eco, U. 161, 163, 165, 171
ethnicity 123, 127, 143, 157
ethnography 25, 46-47, 49, 81-82, 84, 143, 154, 171
ethnoscapes 170
everyday life 18, 20, 65, 86, 92-94, 99, 101, 105-114, 145-146, 148
explosion 35-36

Feuerbach, L. A. 86
Fiske, J. 22, 86, 156
Foucault, M. 55, 58, 134, 161-163
Frankfurt School 16-17, 19, 34-36, 53, 84, 155-156, 159-160
Freud, S. 8, 18, 62-65, 69-70, 75-77, 81-83, 86, 90-91, 114
Freudianism 90

Gadamer, H.-G. 30-31, 57-58, 60-61, 92, 112-113, 126
Geertz, C. 154
Gerbner, G. 163, 166
Giddens, A. 120, 121-122, 142
Gledhill, C. 87
global dialogism 11, 20-21, 119, 124, 140-141
globalization 119-124, 127-131, 133, 137-143, 171
glocalization 121, 139, 141
Grabowicz, G. G. 41
Gramsci, A. 38, 43, 54, 128, 136, 146, 148, 163
grand narrative 97

Index

Habermas, J. 103, 122
Hall, S. 7, 17, 21, 23-26, 29-39, 41-48, 50-51, 53-57, 59-62, 68, 72, 74, 86, 89, 99-100, 109-113, 117, 123, 135-139, 141-143, 145-147, 151-152, 158-159, 168, 171-172
Hartley, J. 13, 15, 27, 86-87
Hebdige, D. 164-165, 167, 171
Hegel, G. W. F. 17-18, 55, 69, 98-99
hegemony 33, 38, 40, 43, 54, 116, 123, 126, 128, 136, 148-149
Heidegger, M. 8, 56-58, 60, 65, 92, 112-113
Held, D. 128
Hoggart, R. 22-24, 47-48, 168
Horkheimer, M. 34, 150, 156, 160
Hymes, D. 154

Ideology 18-20, 29, 32-33, 43-44, 51-56, 58, 60, 62-68, 70-73, 75, 77, 80, 83, 89-90, 93-94, 97-99, 111, 114, 121, 123, 133, 155
Ignatieff, M. 164
implosion 35-36
In-der-Welt-sein 65, 112-113
individual subject 131-132, 135
Ingarten, R. 41
Inglis, F. 16
instinct (Trieb) 63, 65, 75-79, 81, 86, 88, 90, 92, 100, 114, 117
interconnectedness 128

inter-culturality 140-141
interdiscourse 53-54, 57-60, 67-68, 71-75, 100
inter-otherness 140
interpellation 51, 59, 68, 70-75
inter(-)subjectivity 106, 122, 132, 137-141
intertextuality 21, 138
Iser, W. 96, 126, 153-154

Jameson, F. 14, 16, 65, 161-162, 167
Jauss, H. R. 96, 126, 153
Jensen, K. B. 110-111
Jin, H. 8-9, 26, 139, 143, 145-146
Kant, I. 37-38, 135
Katz, E. 126
King, A. D. 143
Konstanz School 153

Lacan, J. 8, 54, 62, 64-65, 69-70, 73, 75-77, 80, 89, 114, 140
Laclau, E. 43, 54, 59-60, 67, 72, 74, 147
Laozi 30, 128
Latour, B. 152, 172
Lenin, V. I. 65, 128
Levinas, E. 55
Liebes, T. 126
lifeworld 110-111
locality 128, 134, 139

MacIntyre, A. 59
Marvin, C. 170-171

Marx, K. 18, 69-70, 83, 86, 91, 99, 133-134
Marxism 19, 24, 36, 66, 79-80, 90, 123, 145, 148, 172
Maslow, H. 82
mass culture 16-18, 34-35, 136, 159, 161
masses 18-19, 34-35, 53, 84, 114, 155-156, 158-160
Matejka, L. 80, 172
material existence 18-20, 66, 88-93, 98-100, 109-110, 114
materiality 66
McCarthy, C. 123, 142-143
McLuhan, M. 150
McQuail, D. 81-82
McRobbie, Angela 141, 143
mediascapes 170
modernity 19, 35, 108, 119-122, 124, 129-130, 132-133, 135-139, 141-142, 162, 171-172
multi-accentuality 155, 162

Nagpal, H. 54
negotiated 26, 29, 33, 39, 41, 68, 73, 113, 136, 158-159
New Labour 148-149
Nietzsche, F. 88, 91, 134
non-viewing 107-109, 113

O'Rourke, R. 48
ontological subject 108
oppositional 26, 29-30, 39, 41-43, 68, 73, 113, 136, 158-159
otherness 90, 127

over-determination 75
Owen, S. 47-48

Parkin, F. 158-159
Pêcheux, M. 53-54, 57, 60, 67-68, 71, 74, 100, 110
Peronist 147
perspectivism 88
phenomenology 95, 110, 126-127
Plekhanov, G. V. 133
political unconscious 14, 65, 114
polysemy 27, 34, 39-41, 46, 49, 56
popular culture 15-17, 23-24, 45, 50, 123, 131, 146-148, 159-160, 164, 167-168
postmodernism 36, 90, 134, 145, 161-162, 164, 167, 172
postmodernity 19, 119-120, 122, 124-125, 127, 129, 132, 135-136, 138-139, 141, 162
poststructuralism 59, 67, 167
producer society 160, 164
psychoanalysis 64-65, 69-70, 72, 75-77, 82-83, 91, 117, 152
public sphere 97

Radway, J. A. 93-94, 153, 172
reception-aesthetics (reception-theory) 26, 96, 125-126, 153
réel 64, 67, 75, 80, 114
representation 33, 64-65, 88, 125, 136, 143
resistance 8, 18-21, 35, 69, 77, 81, 123, 131, 136-137, 158

Rosen, H. 154-155
Rosengren, K. E. 82

Saussure, F. de 32, 155
Scarry, E. 91
Schopenhauer, A. 8, 114, 134
Searle, J. 164
Serres, M. 152, 172
signified 32-33, 134
signifier 32-33, 67, 134-135
Silverstone, R. 93, 104-105, 150, 172
social existence 66, 68, 112-113, 133
social individual 79-81, 83-85, 88, 90, 92, 104, 135
Song-Ming Rationalism 115-116
Spivak, G. C. 140
Storey, J. 16, 23-24, 29, 45-46, 50
structuralism 24, 70, 88-90, 134, 138
subjectivity 40, 52, 106, 122, 127, 130, 134-138, 140, 161
Sznaider, N. 131, 142-143

Thompson, E. P. 23-24
Titunik, I. R. 80, 172
Tomlinson, J. 120-121, 125-127, 130, 132, 136, 139, 143
trans-subjectivity 132
Turner, G. 15, 27-28

Unconscious 8, 14, 63-66, 68-69, 73, 75-77, 83, 90-91, 108, 114
uses and gratifications 78-82

Viewing 94-95, 101, 106-109, 112-113, 123, 166
Vološinov, V. N. 79-80, 85, 155, 161-162, 172

Walkerdine, V. 172
Wang, Yuhui 115
Weedon, C. 48
White, H. 88
Williams, R. 15, 19, 22-25, 48, 92-93, 95, 112-113, 123, 133, 146, 150, 162, 172
Windahl, S. 81-82
Winter, R. 15, 130-133, 136, 141-143
Wolf, M. 163
World-System 143
Wu Jingzi 115-116

Yang Bojun 102

Zhu Xi 37-38